Can It & Ferment It

Can It & Ferment It

More Than 75 Satisfying Small-Batch Canning and
Fermentation Recipes for the Whole Year

Stephanie Thurow

Skyhorse Publishing

Skyhorse Publishing books may be purchased in bulk at special discounts for sales promotion, corporate gifts, fund-raising, or educational purposes. Special editions can also be created to specifications. For details, contact the Special Sales Department, Skyhorse Publishing, 307 West 36th Street, 11th Floor, New York, NY 10018 or info@skyhorsepublishing.com.

Skyhorse® and Skyhorse Publishing® are registered trademarks of Skyhorse Publishing, Inc.®, a Delaware corporation.

Visit our website at www.skyhorsepublishing.com.

10 9 8 7 6 5 4 3 2

Library of Congress Cataloging-in-Publication Data is available on file.

Cover design by Jane Sheppard
Cover photos by Stephanie Thurow

Print ISBN: 978-1-5107-1742-8
Ebook ISBN: 978-1-5107-1743-5

Printed in China

For Sophia

Always know that you can accomplish anything as long as you believe it.
All the strength you need lies within you.

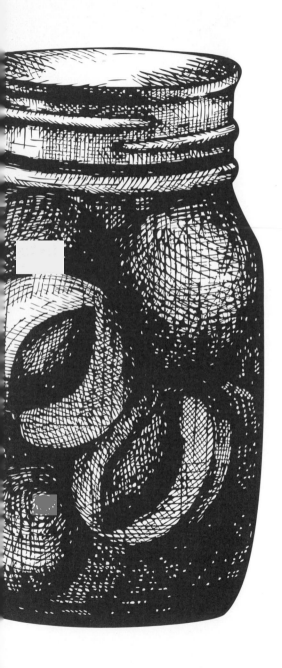

Contents

INTRODUCTION

....

Back in the early 2000s, I thought canning would be a fitting craft to learn because I loved pickles and had been searching for the perfect one to pair with my favorite drink: a Bloody Mary. Though my great-grandmothers were big into canning and fermenting, unfortunately it wasn't something that got passed down through the generations. The only person I knew that canned at the time was my boyfriend's (now husband's) aunt in Wisconsin, Mary. I asked Mary if she'd teach me how to can, and she was more than willing to show me the ins and outs. We set a date to can together in the middle of July, because that's typically when pickling cucumbers are ready in the Midwest.

When the canning weekend finally arrived, I was excited yet nervous for what was in store. Mary had blocked out the entire day for us to can. She explained the importance of using only the freshest ingredients when canning, so we dashed off to our local farmers' market at dawn on a beautiful summer morning. She had a brilliant technique for hauling around all the fresh produce without breaking our backs: use a baby stroller. Mary pulled a dual-seat stroller out of her van, tossed her purse in the underbelly carriage, and high-stepped it into the market. She knew exactly what she was looking for in this moment, and I envied her knowledge and could not wait to soak it up. She squeezed and sniffed produce, seeking out perfectly sized pickling cucumbers (3 inches or smaller, FYI), dill, and onions. When we got back to her house, she explained that we'd have to start by cleaning each of the small pickling cucumbers. Next thing I knew, she rolled out a vintage Wringer Washer from the garage and filled it up with hose water. She tossed a towel in with the cucumbers and agitated the cukes, then drained the water out and refilled it again. She repeated this task until the water ran clear, and wouldn't you know it, those were the cleanest darned cucumbers I'd ever seen. *This woman is a genius*, I thought to myself. We spent the rest of the day perspiring in the kitchen over hot pots of boiling water and brine. She taught me how to pack a pickle jar like nobody's business. To this day, I get compliments on my beautifully packed pickle jars, and I always reply, "I learned from the best!"

I can't remember how many jars of pickles we made that day; too many to count. I know I still had jars on my shelves two years later (and I am a pickle eating machine, so that says a lot). I continued to can with Mary for years; she taught me how to make several different flavors of jam and pickled beets, as well. She cleaned the beets in the Wringer Washer, too! I loved the quality time we'd spend talking about things I would have never otherwise known about her. It was a very special bonding time that I'll always hold dear. That's why when I had my daughter many years later, I knew that I'd want to share this pantry craft and the art of fermentation with her. I hope that it will be a common ground for us now and through the years as we age. Thankfully, she's been a big help in the kitchen since she was one and continues to enjoy cooking with me and her father. I'd love for her to one day pass the knowledge of canning and fermenting down to her children, as I see them as invaluable life skills.

Trying to explain the joy that I have during the process of canning and fermenting food is hard to verbalize, but I'll try: I like to create good-tasting food and share it with family and friends, and of course I love to eat it myself. It is fulfilling to plant seeds in the spring, tend to the garden with my daughter and husband all summer, harvest the gifts from the garden in the fall, and preserve them all year round. Tasting jam made in the spring in the heart of the winter is like taking a mind vacation. I also really like to know what ingredients are going into my food, and I find it ridiculously satisfying to spend an afternoon in the kitchen, stand back when everything is cleaned up, and gaze at my jars of food. I want to enjoy food without the addition of food dyes, artificial preservatives, or other harsh chemicals. After a decade of canning and fermenting, I've learned that a lot of people in the canning and fermentation worlds tend to lean toward one side or the other. I like to can and ferment because both offer completely different flavors and benefits. Why can't we enjoy both? That's why I was inspired to write a book about how to can and ferment the same fruits and vegetables, so you can enjoy the best of both worlds.

Throughout the process of developing recipes and writing this book, I learned a few things:

1. Canning and fermenting is even easier than I originally thought; so many recipes are similar to one another, they just have different variations of salt, water, sugar, vinegar, and seasonings.
2. A majority of the recipes in this book are for pickled vegetables. Though pickling with similar ingredients, each veggie offers a completely different flavor.
3. I really like garlic, like *really* like it, and you must, too, if you are going to enjoy this book (or you can omit it—but what fun is that?).

I have had so many friends and friends of friends ask me to teach them to can, or they have expressed anxiety regarding fermenting food on their own. I understand that as a beginner it seems intimidating, but I am here to tell you that it's easier than you think. Once you get the hang of it, you'll wish you had started years ago. Each recipe has been tested and retested. I've tried to write the recipes in this book in a very basic format to put you at ease. But trust me, if you mess up, it's okay. We learn from our mistakes. I've included a notes section on every recipe because I want you to use my recipes as a jumping-off point for future creations as you get more confident. If you make a change to a recipe, write it down and take note because chances are that a year later when you go to make the recipe again, you won't remember how you made it. If you don't like the finished product, take note of that too and consider options to tweaking it to your liking in the future.

This book will not educate you on the extensive history of canning and fermenting food, nor will it go into the detailed stages that the food goes through during the fermentation process. While there are plenty of great resources out there that dive deep into those topics, this book will get right down to the business of preserving. All canning recipes in this book are water bath recipes; no pressure cooker recipes. There are no recipes for bread, wine, kombucha, or beer, just fruit and vegetables that can be canned as well as fermented. None of the fermented recipes require a starter culture or whey. Most of this cookbook contains small-batch recipes that will yield a couple of pints or a few quarts, and I wrote it this way for two reasons: because some people don't have a lot of space to store a lot of jarred foods, and because it gives you an opportunity to try out a recipe and determine if you like it without investing a lot of time or money. If you enjoy a particular recipe, double or triple it the next time you make it.

This book is broken down into three main sections: spring, summer, and fall/winter. I have included canning and fermentation recipes using my favorite fruits and vegetables to preserve during each season. Fall and winter kind of overlap each other, which is why I decided to combine them into one section. There are also recipe variations and a few guest recipes submitted by fermentation industry pros throughout the chapters. I hope you find this book to be inspirational and educational, and I hope it proves to be an excellent guide for your food preservation endeavors.

Each recipe is marked with an icon to indicate method. The mason jar indicates canning, and the head of cabbage indicates fermentation.

CANNING AND FERMENTATION: EXPLAINING THE DIFFERENCES

Water bath canning: allows us to preserve food with freshness and flavor after going through the high-heat process of a boiling water bath. This method of preservation creates an airtight, high-acid environment in which bacteria and other harmful contaminates cannot survive. Through this preservation process, canned goods become shelf-stable and can be stored in a pantry or cupboard for up to a year.

Ferments: foods that are fermented in salt or a saltwater brine. The process of vegetable fermentation creates an acidic environment by converting sugar into acid in which bad or unsafe bacteria cannot survive. This is known as lactic acid fermentation, more popularly called lacto-fermenation. The process of fermentation can take days, weeks, months, or even years depending on the flavor desired and the specific fruit or vegetable used. The recipes in this book generally take only a few days or weeks.

The studies on fermented foods are endless and truly fascinating to read. If you haven't already, I encourage you to take some time to research the topic and the health benefits linked to fermented food. Refer to the Resources section of this book (p. 173) for recommended reading.

The importance of local and organic produce: ferment or can with the freshest available fruits and vegetables whenever possible; they are going to have the best flavor if they are picked at their peak and will retain more nutritional value compared to produce from the grocery store. Most produce sold at the grocery store is picked long before it's ripe, so by the time it reaches store shelves, it's lost much of its vitamins and nutrients. Per the USDA National Institute of Food and Agriculture, produce that is canned promptly after harvest can be more nutritious than fresh produce sold in local stores. The USDA goes on to say that within one to two weeks, even refrigerated produce loses half or more of some of its vitamins.

I always try to find produce at the farmers' market that has been harvested the day of or the day prior; that way I preserve the produce within 24–48 hours of when it's harvested.

Use organic produce whenever possible and always use produce that is not treated with a food-grade wax sealant or harsh chemicals. In addition to using freshly harvested foods, be sure to pick fruits and vegetables that are not bruised or damaged. I also recommend trying and selecting produce that's uniform in size. Having uniformity allows the food to pickle/ferment evenly, which will result in a consistent end product.

I have found that most farmers are happy to explain their farming practices and that many of their produce items are often farmed organically, but the farmers have not gone through the process of making that official due to the cost incurred. Do not be shy to ask your farmer questions about the way they farm, because you might be pleasantly surprised by their answers. Be sure to always ask when produce was harvested to ensure freshness.

CANNING SUPPLIES

Salt: for water bath canning. Canning salt, also known as pickling salt, is preferred; it is pure sodium chloride. Kosher salt is also acceptable, though the amounts may vary. Be sure to check a salt conversion chart. You can find one at mortonsalt.com/article/salt-conversion-chart/. Never use iodized salt.

Vinegar: only use vinegars that indicate a 5–6 percent acidity level. Many will note "pickling vinegar" on the packaging. I've personally only used store-bought vinegar because it offers reliable results and I know it's safe. For the sake of simplicity, every recipe in this cookbook will call for 5 percent acidity, distilled white vinegar, or organic apple cider vinegar.

Water: the purest water you have available to you is the best option. I have a reverse osmosis system at home from which I use water quite often. Water with minerals such as iron could cause discoloration. I've canned with tap water for many years, and it's worked great with the water from the city where I live. If you are in a rural area and have well water as your main source, you can have the water tested to see if there has been any contamination. If you are unsure, store-bought water is an option.

Lemon juice: a couple of recipes in this book call for lemon juice. Use fresh juice from lemons or store-bought lemon juice but know that it is ideal to use store-bought lemon juice when canning, since the acidity level is reliable when compared to using fresh lemons.

Common Canning Supplies
- A large water bath canning pot with lid and a rack, 21–33 quarts big. These are typically sold in big box stores in a starter set or online. The rack is required to keep jars off the bottom of the pot but also to allow water to flow around all sides of the jars. Canning pots range from about $20 to $100. Read the range recommendations for each water bath canner; some do not work with electric, glass-top ranges.
- A stainless steel wide-mouth funnel.
- Glass jars. I use two main types of jars when canning: one is a standard Mason-style home-canning jar (in either quart, pint, or half-pint size) with a BPA-free self-sealing lid and metal ring. Always use new lids; never reuse lids when water bath sealing. The other type of jar I commonly use is an all-glass jar with a rubber seal and glass lid. These

jars also have two metal clamps that clip the jar shut. Be sure to only use glass jars that are specifically made to withstand high heat when canning such as Ball, Kerr, and Weck jars. For simplicity, all recipes in this book call for standard wide or regular mouth Mason-style home-canning jars in 32 oz., 16 oz., or 8 oz. variations.

- Canning tongs or a jar lifter to insert and remove jars from the hot water bath.
- A stainless-steel potato masher, used when making jam.
- A stainless-steel ladle.
- Measuring cups. I have a selection of 1-, 2-, 4-, and 8-cup measuring cups, and I use them all.
- Measuring spoons in a variety of sizes.
- Clean lint-free towels and paper towels.
- A sharp paring knife.
- A stainless-steel butter knife, used for hot and cold packing of jars.
- Large and medium-sized thick-bottomed, nonreactive (stainless-steel or enamel-lined) pots for making jams, sauces, and brine. For many years, I used wide-bottomed, large pans I had around the house for jam, but after I committed to the realization that I loved canning and it would be something I make year after year, I invested in a Kilner Stainless-Steel Jam Pot. It runs about $100, which is nothing to bat an eye at, but it does make canning life easier. It's a high-quality 8.45-quart stainless-steel pot that has measurements inside the pot. It also has handles, which simplifies pouring. It's not a required pot for canning, but if you decide that making jam is your jam, consider adding it to your wish list.
- Candy thermometer, to measure the temperature of the water or jam sauce (not required for any of the recipes in the book, but convenient to have on hand when canning or if you want to test the temperature to be on the safe side).
- Occasionally throughout the book, a food processor, mandolin slicer, or hand blender would streamline the process in some recipes. These are not required for canning but very helpful to have around when needed.

Disclaimer: the USDA recommends using plastic utensils when canning; however, I personally only use stainless steel, as I do not like to heat plastic. I've never had a jar break from using stainless steel, but if you are leery, feel free to use plastic funnel, ladles, and other utensils.

CANNING PROCESS: STEP-BY-STEP

1.

Simmer new lids in a small saucepan until ready to use.

2.

Keep empty jars in hot water bath until use.

3.

Use a funnel to safely transfer the hot brine/liquid into the jar.

4.

Fill jars, leaving ¼ or ½ inch headspace (varies per recipe).

5.

Wipe the rim of the jar with a clean, dampened, lint-free cloth or paper towel and again with a dry towel.

6.

Place the canning lid onto the jar and twist the canning ring on until just-snug.

7.

Use canning tongs to carefully place jars into the water bath. Once all jars are in the water bath, cover the water bath canner with the lid and, once it begins to boil, set the timer.

8.

Submerge filled jars in hot water bath.

9.

Once processed, carefully remove the hot jars from the water bath using the canning tongs. I recommend using a dish towel to hold under the jar to transfer the hot jars from the water bath to the counter or table. Allow the processed jars to cool on a towel-covered surface for up to 12 hours. Do not touch the jars or test the lids for 12 or more hours after processing.

CANNING PROCESS

Hot Pack versus Cold Pack

There are two main ways to fill jars when canning. The hot pack method is when a jar is filled with hot, precooked food such as jam. The cold pack method is when a jar is filled with uncooked produce and the fruit or veggies are covered with a hot liquid brine or syrup. The liquid needs to be hot during this process; otherwise, there is a risk of the jar breaking during the water bath process. A broken jar will happen to the best of us, but it's never a good feeling. All contents of the broken or cracked jar must be carefully disposed of and cannot be reused. Both methods of cold and hot packing result in sealing the jars via the boiling hot water bath method. It's important to always leave headspace in the jars; this book will call for ¼ to ½ inches of space between the top of the liquid or food and the rim of the jar. The amount of space varies from recipe to recipe throughout the book. This extra space allows for expansion of the food in the jar during the sealing process. When packing jars with fruits and veggies, it's important to try and remove any air bubbles trapped within the contents of the jar to reduce the risk of spoilage. I use a stainless-steel chopstick to aid in removing bubbles when packing hot and cold packs, but a stainless-steel butter knife works just as well.

The Process of Boiling

Water bath canning involves submerging filled jars in a boiling hot water bath. This process kills bacteria that might otherwise cause spoilage and creates a vacuum that removes air from jars and seals them tightly to prevent any outside contamination. Water bath canning allows for long-term storage without refrigeration.

When canning, always check the rims of jars to make sure there are no cracks or chips. Jars and rings may be reused, but lids should always be brand new. High acid preserves that are water bath canned 10 minutes or longer do not require the jars to be sterilized first. Every canning recipe in this book will be processed 10 minutes or longer, but you should wash all jars with soap and rinse thoroughly. I use a dishwasher to clean my jars and lids at the same time; I leave them in the dishwasher to keep warm until I'm ready to fill them. If you do not have a dishwasher, you must heat your jars after washing to keep them warm before filling. The National Center for Home Preservation recommends submerging the jars in hot water, right-side up in the pot, with water 1 inch above the jars.

Turn the heat up once submerged and allow the jars to simmer until you are ready to fill them with food. Use canning tongs to remove the jars from the water, cautiously dump out the hot water back into the pot, and carefully set the jars on a clean towel and allow them to cool slightly. Use a small saucepan to simmer canning lids until they are ready to be used, then set them out on a clean towel or napkin to dry. Jars should remain warm until they are ready to fill. If you use a dishwasher, they can be kept warm inside until the food is ready to be canned. Keeping the jars warm will help avoid breakage of the jars from what is called "thermal shock," which can occur when there is a large temperature difference.

Fill water bath canner with water and bring to a boil. The size of jars being sealed will determine how much water to add to the canning pot. If you use small half-pint, 8-ounce jars, the pot only needs to be filled up about halfway (depending on the height of the rack). You must keep in mind that once the jars are added to the pot, the water line will rise. You want the water to cover the submerged jars by about 1 inch when you begin the boiling water bath processing time.

After filling the jars to the recommended amount per recipe (either leaving ¼ or ½ inches of headspace), use a stainless-steel butter knife or other nonreactive tool to remove any air bubbles trapped within the jar (if needed). Next, use a slightly dampened lint-free towel or paper towel to clean the lip of the jar. Remove any droppings of food or liquid and wipe again with a dry paper towel. You want the area of the jar that the lid will lie on to be clean. Place the canning lid on the jar with the sealing side touching the jar and gently twist the ring over the lid. The ring should not be firmly tightened on the jar, but should be "just snug" or tightened until you begin to feel resistance. It is recommended to read the instructions that come with the canning lids if you have never canned before, to get a good idea of how much to tighten the lid. If the ring is tightened too much, it can cause the jars to break; on the other hand, if it is not tightened enough, the jar may not seal properly. Once the water bath is ready, use the canning tongs (jar lifter) to carefully transfer the jars into the hot water bath; make sure to keep the jar level.

Preheat the boiling-water-bath canner before starting the process of food prep. It can take quite a while to heat the large pot of water. Bring the canning pot to a rolling boil while you prepare the food for canning. I have a habit of lowering the temperature of my water bath right before I add my jars. I canned for eight years without ever breaking a jar, and suddenly I broke my first three jars in the same canning session. I was devastated and confused as to why I was breaking jars now and never had before. Then it dawned on me by the third break that my new stove was running *much* hotter than my old one. So, to be on the safe side, once my water bath heats up to boiling, I turn it down just a little until it stops the hard rolling boil, then I put my jars in and turn the heat back up until it's a rolling boil again. Once the water bath starts boiling, cover the pot and begin the processing timer.

Sea level plays a factor in how long you will seal your jars in the water bath. All recipes in this book are based on processing at an elevation of up to 1,000 feet above sea level. Anything over that will require more processing time. If you are 1,001 ft. or more above sea level, please refer to the chart below and add minutes to processing time as needed.

1,001–3,000 ft.	Add 5 minutes to processing time
3,001–6,000 ft.	Add 10 minutes to processing time
6,000–8,000 ft.	Add 15 minutes to processing time
8,001–10,000 ft.	Add 20 minutes to processing time

Once the processing time ends, turn the heat to low and let the water settle down for a few minutes. Then, using the canning tongs (jar lifter), carefully lift the jars out of the hot water bath and transfer them to a towel-covered counter or table where they will not be disturbed for 12 hours. After 12 hours, remove the rings from the jars and test each jar to make sure they are sealed. If a jar does not seal after 12 hours, you can keep it in the refrigerator. Never eat anything that does not smell right. Use your instincts if something does not look right or smell right. Like my grandpa always says, "When in doubt, throw it out!"

Store sealed canned goods in a dark, dry, and cool place. Keep the metal rings off the canned goods while they are in storage to prevent jars from exploding (on the off chance that something did not seal properly). We have an old well in our home that the previous owners covered and built wall shelves on to store canned goods. It's the perfect spot to keep the sealed preserves; organized, dark, and cool. If you don't have a basement or a space like this, put them on the bottom shelf of a cupboard. Refrain from storing the jars up high, as heat rises. According to the USDA, it is best to store your goods between 50 and 70°F. You do not want to display them in a location where they get direct sunlight. Sunlight can cause the color and flavor of your preserves to change, and it can also deplete nutrients from the canned goods.

Refrigerate all canned goods after breaking the seal. Fruit-based preserves will last two months after opening and vinegar-based preserves are best consumed within six months.

Each recipe in this book has a suggested yield. The amount made per recipe can vary due to the size of fruits/vegetables used. I recommend preparing one or two extra jars in case a recipe makes more than the suggested yield. Jars not full enough to be water bath sealed can be cooled and stored in the refrigerator in an airtight container.

FERMENTATION SUPPLIES

Salt: for the purpose of simplicity, every recipe in this book calls for kosher salt. Sea salt is a great option for fermenting, but the amounts vary due to the fine grain of sea salt. Refer to a salt conversion chart like www.mortonsalt.com/article/salt-conversion-chart/ when using alternate salt options. Table salt is not recommended.

Water: the purest water you have available to you is the best option. I have a reverse osmosis system at home from which I use water quite often. Water with minerals such as iron could cause discoloration. Some chemicals added to city water, such as chlorine, could possibly cause an adverse reaction to the end product, but you may need to learn by trial and error to know if your tap water will work. If you are in a rural area and have well water as your main source, you can have the water tested to see if there has been any contamination. If you are unsure, store-bought water is an option.

Common Fermentation Supplies

- Measuring cups. I have a selection of 1-, 2-, 4-, and 8-cup measuring cups, and I use them all.
- Measuring spoons in a variety of sizes.
- Clean lint-free towels or paper towels.
- A sharp knife.
- Glass jars. I prefer wide mouth jars for most recipes. I use two main types of jars when I can/ferment. One is a standard canning jar (in either quart or pint size) with a BPA-free lid and metal ring, and the other is a glass jar with a rubber gasket and a glass lid. These jars also have two metal clamps that clip the jar shut.
- Cheese cloth (or other breathable cover) and rubber binders or metal jar rings if using a Mason-style canning jar.
- A fermentation crock.
- Weights.
- Cutting board.
- A vegetable shredder: optional but helpful.
- A wooden kraut pounder/masher/damper: optional but helpful.

There are many different fermentation vessels on the market as of late. It's great that the fermentation movement is rolling full bore, but the list of options can get overwhelming for beginners. For that reason, I use small crocks and Mason-type jars for the recipes in this book. However, in my personal life I use a variety of fermentation vessels because I prefer different styles for different foods. For example, when I ferment hot peppers, I prefer to use an all-glass jar with lid and airlock and small glass weight. For making sauerkraut, I always use a crock, sometimes one with a water seal and sometimes without. I have included a list of different fermentation vessels that I have personal experience using. Just know that fermenting does not have to be complicated or expensive, Mason-style canning jars work just fine.

Mason-style jars are great for small-batch ferments for most fruit and vegetable recipes throughout this book.

Crocks come in all different shapes and sizes, but these are the crocks I most commonly use in my daily life. Small crocks are great for testing recipes or making small batches. Large crocks are wonderful because they yield a lot and ferment large batches at once. Crocks with a water seal are great because the lid protects against bug or dust contamination and keeps the air out. The water seal creates a natural airlock that prevents against mold, yeast, and other harmful bacteria from spoiling the ferment. It's very hands-free in some regard because it does not have to be tended to as frequently as vessels without a water seal and it allows the carbon dioxide that is created during fermentation to release on its own. The two other crocks are handmade and come with a lid/weight that fits inside of the crock, which is wonderful for keeping fermenting food pushed down under the brine. An additional weight is typically needed for this style. Never use a reactive metal such as aluminum when fermenting. Food-grade plastic is a safe alternative, but the previously mentioned vessels are personally what I prefer. Check Resources (p. 173) to see where to find crocks and other fermentation supplies like the ones referenced above.

Some jars come with airlocks or have airlocks you can twist onto a standard home canning jar. These jars do a fantastic job of keeping the ferment airtight and release the carbon dioxide without having to be "burped" on a daily basis.

I have a variety of Weck Jars, which are all glass with glass lids; I use these jars for both canning and fermenting. I have found that the various sized lids are excellent weights. Even though they aren't super heavy, they *usually* do a fabulous job of holding down my small-batch Mason jar ferments. Sometimes I need to use two glass lids to create enough weight to keep the ferment under the brine.

The cabbage shredder and sauerkraut pounder/masher/damper are totally optional tools when making sauerkraut, but they make the process much easier. The shredder makes a nice thin shred of cabbage and exponentially speeds up the shredding process.

Note on cleanliness

Before fermenting, run your supplies through the dishwasher or hand wash them with soapy water. No need to sanitize tools or vessels when fermenting. Wooden fermenting supplies generally don't require soap, but check the directions that come with the particular product to learn the proper care techniques.

Throughout the cookbook, I suggest ways to ferment each recipe. I vary between using a mason jar (sometimes with the canning lid and ring tightly twisted on and sometimes covered with a cheese cloth or other breathable cover), a fermentation crock, and occasionally a glass jar with an airlock. Please realize that everything can be fermented in a Mason-style canning jar, if that is what you have on hand, and everything could be fermented with a jar with airlock or in a crock. Please do not feel that you are required to ferment in the vessels noted: it's just a suggestion.

FERMENTATION PROCESS

Fermented foods are generally made at room temperature, and salt is often used to control the spoilage. Salt helps the probiotic or healthy-belly bacteria grow and creates lactic acid by breaking down the sugars in the food. The benefits of probiotic bacteria are not comparable to commercially processed foods. Because the fermentation process already starts to break down the food, it's easier for the body to digest, as well. The tangy and sour flavor of fermented food cannot be compared to anything else because the process of fermentation creates a unique and delicious taste that cannot be mimicked.

Brine level plays a crucial role in the success of a ferment. The brine always needs to be over the fruit or vegetable that is fermenting by about ¼ inch and no more than 1 inch. This keeps air out of the ferment and prevents mold from forming.

Remove floaters. If you notice small pieces of fruit or vegetable floating up to the surface and hanging out on the top of your brine, use a clean stainless-steel or wooden spoon to scoop out the floater. Floaters make the ferment more susceptible to molding if left, though I've found this isn't an issue when I use an airlock system or crock with a water seal.

Temperature is a huge factor in proper fermentation. As noted in all the fermented recipes in this book, 60 to 75°F is the best range for proper fermentation. Keep in mind that the warmer the room is, the quicker fermentation will happen; and, adversely, the colder a room is, the slower the fruit or vegetable will ferment. I try to keep my house between 68 and 72°F year-round, as this is the hot spot range for ferments in my experience. I love kimchi more than anyone I've met, but I do not like making kimchi in the summer when the kitchen is warm because it ferments too quickly and tastes overly sour. This is a turnoff to *me*, but you may like it better that way. I make sauerkraut year-round, but in the summer, I ferment it for three weeks instead of the five weeks I do in the wintertime. If you do not have air conditioning in the summer, consider leaving a covered ferment in the basement (if you have one). Otherwise, plan to do most of your fermenting during the cooler months of the year. You could always ask to keep your ferments at a friend's; I've done it!

Check on your ferments at least once a day for short-duration fermented recipes and every few days for long-duration ferments, such as sauerkraut. Check in on them to make sure the brine remains over the fruit/vegetables. Some recipes throughout the book require burping a ferment, which needs to be done daily or multiple times throughout the day. When checking on ferments, you are also looking to make sure no mold or yeast is developing.

Burping the ferment is required in a couple recipes throughout the book, such as the Fermented Cranberry-Orange Relish (p. 127) and Cherry Tomatoes with Garlic and Fresh Basil (p. 99). During the process of fermentation, carbon dioxide is produced and needs to be released to avoid gas buildup and cracking or exploding jars. Water-sealed crocks keep air out of the crock and allow the gas to release on its own, which is very convenient and preferred for certain ferments like sauerkraut.

Cloudy brine and sediment are completely normal and a good thing! When your brine ferments start going through the fermentation process, the brine color will change from clear to cloudy. When you are fermenting beets, for example, the brine will turn a deep, dark purple. In some ferments, you'll see a white sediment on the ferment or at the bottom of the jar. This is all a normal part of the fermentation process.

Kahm yeast is a white, thin, powdery-looking film of yeast that grows on the surface of ferments. It's not harmful but has a strong flavor that most people do not like. If caught early, it's easy to remove by dabbing with a paper towel or scooping out with a spoon. If the yeast is mixed in with your brine, it can cause the taste of the ferment to change. Determine if the kahm yeast has spoiled your ferment by taste testing.

Tannins are naturally occurring in grape leaves, raspberry leaves, oak leaves, and cherry leaves, and they help keep fermented pickles crunchy. Freeze a few leaves in order to always have them on hand when needed.

INCLUDE THE CHILDREN!

My daughter has liked to help in the kitchen since she was about eighteen months old. As she's grown, her ability to help has increased tremendously. She's been able to prepare a delicious batch of bone broth since she was five and can scramble eggs like the best of 'em! Here is a list of suggested tasks that children can do to help can and ferment. Little will they know they are learning priceless lessons about food preservation!

Ages 1–3

- Pour measured-out ingredients into jars/pots
- Rinse off fruits and vegetables
- Break apart cauliflower florets with hands for Fermented Giardiniera (p. 143)
- Taste and smell ingredients and seasonings
- Pick dandelion flowers for Dandelion Jelly (p. 52)
- Pick seeds out of the pumpkin in Sugar Pumpkin Kvass (p. 131) and Fermented Butternut Squash (p. 164)

Ages 4–5

- Stir salt into water to dissolve it
- Crank the handle of the apple peeler-corer
- Using a child-safe plastic serrated knife, children can cut soft fruits and veggies into pieces
- Use a cherry pitter to pit cherries (very fun!)
- Stir ingredients together
- Mash fruit, such as strawberries for Chunky Strawberry Sauce (p. 44)

- Pound cabbage shreds into the crock using hands or a cabbage pounder
- Pick dandelion buds for Fermented Dandelion Buds (p. 55)
- Peel garlic

Ages 6+

- Use a real knife to carefully cut vegetables and fruit into uniform size pieces
- Scrub produce clean, such as pickling cucumbers
- Measure out ingredients
- Read recipes
- Stir hot ingredients over stove
- Peel skin off beets for Grandma's Pickled Beets (p. 100)

SPRING

NOTES

STRAWBERRY RHUBARB JAM

The combination of strawberries and rhubarb together is a duo like none other. The sweetness of the strawberries paired with the sour of the rhubarb is a match made in heaven. This jam is not only delicious smothered on a piece of toast, but it's also great on top of pancakes, with cream cheese and graham crackers (a perfect snack for kids and a household favorite), or on top of ice cream! To have rhubarb on hand year-round, clean, chop, and freeze 4 bags of it. When you are ready to make more jam, just pull out the frozen rhubarb a day ahead and prepare the recipe as you would with fresh rhubarb.

....

Yield: 3 pints or 6 (8 oz.) jars

5 cups (1½ pounds) strawberries, stems removed, quartered
4 cups (6–8 stalks) rhubarb, chopped into ½-inch slices
¼ cup lemon juice
1 cup water
3 cups organic or non-GMO sugar (or 2 cups honey)

Wash berries and rhubarb well. Once all berries are quartered, use a potato masher to break down the strawberries into a chunky consistency. Put all ingredients in a large thick-bottomed pot and mix well.

Bring mixture to a boil and reduce to a medium-high heat. Simmer 15 to 20 minutes and stir often to avoid burning the jam. Watch out for flyaway jam splatter—it hurts! If you have a candy thermometer, the temperature you want to reach for is 220°F. Once the sauce has thickened, turn the heat down to low. If the jam does not get hot enough, the result will be more of a sauce-like consistency versus a thick jam—with the same great taste.

Ladle the hot strawberry rhubarb mixture into prepared jars and use a funnel to safely transfer the sauce, leaving ¼ inch of headspace. Wipe the rims of the jars with a clean, dampened, lint-free cloth or paper towel and once again with a dry towel, to remove any jam or liquid from the rim of the jar. Place the canning lid on the jar and twist on the canning ring until it's just-snug on the jar. Carefully transfer the jars into the water bath using the canning tongs. Process in the water bath for 10 minutes. Carefully remove the jars from the water bath with the canning tongs and place jars on a towel for 12 hours without touching. Store in the refrigerator after breaking the seal.

RHUBARB APPLE JAM

The apple and rhubarb blend together seamlessly to create this delicious jam that can be enjoyed with cheese, bread, or pork dishes. Turn this into a fall flavor by adding ½ tsp. ground cinnamon.

....

Yield: 3 pints or 6 (8 oz.) jars

5 cups (10 stalks) rhubarb, sliced into ½-inch pieces
3–4 (4 cups) organic apples, peeled, cored, diced
1 cup water
¼ cup lemon juice
3 cups organic or non-GMO sugar

In a heavy-bottomed saucepan, mix together all the ingredients and bring to a boil. Lower temperature to medium-high heat and simmer for 15 minutes. Stir often to avoid burning the jam. Be careful not to get burned by flyaway jam splatter—it hurts! If you have a candy thermometer, the temperature you want to reach for is 220°F. Once the sauce thickens, turn the heat down to low.

Ladle the hot apple rhubarb mixture into prepared jars. Use a funnel to safely transfer the sauce, leaving ¼ inch of headspace. Wipe the rims of the jars with a clean, damp, lint-free cloth or paper towel and once again with a dry cloth, removing any jam or liquid from the rim of the jar. Place the lid on the jar and twist the canning ring on until it's just-snug on the jar. Carefully transfer the jars into the water bath. Process in the water bath for 10 minutes. Carefully remove the jars from the water bath with the canning tongs and place jars on a towel for 12 hours without touching. Store in the refrigerator after breaking the seal.

NOTES

RHUBARB PICKLES

The leaves of the rhubarb plant are poisonous; do not use them in the ferment.

....

Yield: 1 quart

5–6 ribs rhubarb, thin stalks
   are preferred as they are
   more tender
1 tsp. coriander seeds
1 shallot, quartered
1 bay leaf

Brine:

1 tbsp. kosher salt, dissolved
   in 2 cups of water

Wash the rhubarb stalks well and trim off the leaves and ends. Use the quart-sized jar to measure the length you want to cut your rhubarb. I recommend cutting it 2 inches below the top of the jar to leave space for the brine and weight.

Add the coriander seeds to the bottom of the jar, then carefully pack the jar with the rhubarb spears, shallot, and bay leaf. Be gentle with the bay leaf, as you do not want it to crumble.

Pour brine over the rhubarb. Use a weight to hold the vegetables underneath the brine. Cover your jar or crock with a cheese cloth or other breathable cover to keep dust and bugs from entering your ferment. Store at room temperature, ideally between 60 and 75°F. If you are using a clear jar, keep out of direct sunlight or wrap a dish towel around the jar.

This is a 2-week ferment. Be sure to check on the ferment every few days to make sure the brine remains over the rhubarb and that no mold or yeast forms. If the brine is low, press down the weight to bring the brine back over the ferment. Once fermentation is complete, store in an airtight glass jar and refrigerate.

NOTES

GARLICKY ASPARAGUS

These salty, garlicky spears make a wonderful replacement for any regular dill pickle. They are a beautiful addition to a relish platter and a perfect garnish in a Bloody Mary. Medium-sized asparagus spears are ideal for this recipe. The skinny spears risk becoming too tender, and the thick spears take up a lot of room in the jars.

······················

Yield: 2 quarts

3 lb. (about 60 spears) fresh asparagus

8 cloves garlic, quartered

2 tsp. dried dill seeds

2 tsp. yellow mustard seeds

2 tbsp. red pepper flakes (optional)

Brine:

3 cups (5 percent acidity) distilled white vinegar

3 cups water

¼ cup pickling salt

Clean the asparagus thoroughly, trim off the ends to fit the canning jar (cut to about 6 inches if using a quart jar). Ball brand makes a tall glass jar that is great for asparagus. Weck Jars is another brand I often use when pickling asparagus because they offer all-glass cylindrical jars in various sizes. Basic canning quart jars will work just as well, but the spears will be shorter than they would be in a taller jar. If taller jars are used, prepare more brine to fill the larger jars.

In a nonreactive pot, bring the brine ingredients to a boil and simmer for 3 minutes. Divide the garlic, dill seeds, mustard seeds, and pepper flakes (optional) between the prepared canning jars. Pack the jars with asparagus as tightly as possible, without bruising or damaging the spears.

Ladle the hot brine over the spears and use a funnel to safely transfer the brine into the jars. Leave ½ inches of headspace. Wipe the rims of the jars with a dampened, clean, lint-free cloth or paper towel and then again with a dry towel and place the canning lid on. Twist the canning ring on until it's just-snug on the jar. Process in the water bath for 10 minutes. Carefully remove the jars from the water bath with the canning tongs and place jars on a towel for 12 hours without touching. Though the asparagus will have immediate flavor, they are best if they pickle for 4 weeks or longer before tasting. Store in the refrigerator after breaking the seal.

GARLICKY ASPARAGUS

Children may not like roasted or grilled asparagus, but I've never had one turn down a fermented garlic asparagus pickle!

....

Yield: 1 quart or taller jar if you'd like to keep them whole

1 ½ lb. asparagus, uniform in thickness if possible
½ tsp. dried dill seeds, or a sprig of fresh dill
½ tsp. yellow mustard seeds
1 bay leaf
2 garlic cloves, halved

Brine:

1 tbsp. kosher salt, dissolved in 2 cups of water

As with water bath canned asparagus, I prefer to use medium-sized spears. Clean the asparagus thoroughly and trim off the ends to fit into your jar/fermentation vessel. Add dill and mustard seeds to the bottom of the jar and begin to pack the jar with the asparagus. Gently tuck the bay leaf and garlic within the spears.

Pour the brine over the asparagus and add a weight to hold the vegetables under the brine.

Cover jar/crock with a cheese cloth or other breathable cover to keep dust and bugs from entering your ferment. Store at room temperature, ideally between 60 and 75°F. If you are using a clear jar, keep it out of direct sunlight or wrap a dish towel around the jar to keep the light out.

This is an 8-day ferment. Check on the ferment daily. I have noticed that kahm yeast always tends to show up if I'm not actively checking on my asparagus ferment. Though the yeast is harmless, I dislike the flavor very much. It is a white film that tends to show up, and if caught early on, it can be removed with a paper towel very easily without disturbing your ferment. If the brine is not covering the tips of the asparagus, be sure to push the weight down to bring the brine level back over the vegetable. Once fermentation is complete, store in an airtight glass jar and refrigerate.

Recipe Variation: Basic Garlicky Asparagus

2 garlic cloves

Brine:

1 tbsp. kosher salt, dissolved in 2 cups of water

Follow the recipe as written, but add two cloves of garlic to the bottom of the jar and pack it up with asparagus—so simple but so delicious!

WHOLE CHERRIES IN HONEY SYRUP

These cherries are fantastic straight from the jar but are also tasty garnishes in cocktails and wonderful additions to yogurt, smoothies, ice cream, and oatmeal. Sweet or sour cherries can be used for this recipe. If using a sour cherry, consider making the heavier, sweeter syrup variation of the recipe. If you are using a sweet cherry, consider using the lighter variation.

....

Yield: 4 regular-mouth jars

1 pound cherries, stems removed, pitted (A cherry pitter speeds up the process exponentially and is fun to use! Cherry pitters are easy tools for children to manipulate and do not have any sharp, knife-like parts.)

Light syrup:

2 cups water
¾ cup honey

Heavy syrup:

2 cups water
1½ cups honey

Prepare cherries. In a heavy-bottomed saucepan, heat water and honey over medium-high heat until the honey is dissolved. Simmer for 5 minutes. Pack jars with the cherries.

Ladle the hot syrup over the fresh cherries. Use a funnel to safely transfer the syrup into the jar and leave ½ inch of headspace. Check for pockets of air trapped between the cherries, syrup, and the glass jar. Use a stainless-steel butter knife or other tool to remove air bubbles. Wipe the rims of the jars with a dampened, clean, lint-free cloth or paper towel and then again with a dry towel. Place the canning lid on each jar and twist the canning ring on until it's just-snug on the jar. Process in the water bath for 25 minutes. Carefully remove jars from the water bath with the canning tongs and place them on a towel for 12 hours without touching. Refrigerate after breaking the seal.

Sugar Syrup Variation

Light:

2 cups water
1 cup non-GMO or organic sugar

Heavy:

2 cups water
1½ cups non-GMO or organic sugar

NOTES

CHERRY SALSA

This salsa is a lovely sweet and spicy springtime treat for a variety of occasions. It's a great accompaniment to chips or on tacos, but my favorite is on top of scrambled eggs!

....

Yield: 1 quart

3 cups cherries, seeded, chopped

1 jalapeno, chopped (omit seeds and membranes if you want less spice)

1 cup cilantro, chopped

1½ tsp. (about 1 lime) fresh lime juice

⅓ cup red onion, finely chopped

1 tbsp. kosher salt

Mix the prepared ingredients together, pack into a clean quart jar or fermentation vessel of choice, and weigh down mixture with a weight. Make sure the juices completely cover the chopped mixture.

If using a canning jar, tightly screw on a canning lid and ring. Store at room temperature, ideally between 60 and 75°F. If you are using a clear jar, keep it out of direct sunlight or wrap a dish towel around the jar to keep the light out.

Fruit-based ferments do not take as long as vegetables to ferment. Taste test this recipe after 24 hours to determine if you'd like to ferment another 12 or 24 additional hours. I prefer the flavor after fermenting for 36 hours. Once fermentation is complete, store in an airtight glass jar and refrigerate for up to two weeks.

NOTES

CHUNKY STRAWBERRY SAUCE

Strawberry sauce is a great addition to an ice cream sundae, pancakes, waffles (mixed into the batter), or added to lemonade on a hot summer day.

....

Yield: 2 pints

2 lb. strawberries, stems removed, quartered

4 cups non-GMO or organic sugar

¼ cup lemon juice

In a wide bowl, use a potato masher to crush strawberries in batches until you have 3 cups of mashed berries. Leave strawberries more intact if you prefer more chunkiness.

In a heavy-bottomed saucepan, mix together the strawberries, sugar, and lemon juice. Stir over low heat until the sugar is dissolved, then increase the heat to high and bring the mixture to a full rolling boil. Be sure to stir often to avoid burning the mixture. Continue stirring and cooking for 15 minutes so the liquid can cook down into a thicker sauce-like consistency.

Ladle the sauce into a prepared jar. Use a funnel to safely transfer the sauce, leaving ¼ inch of headspace. Wipe the rims of the jars with a dampened, clean, lint-free cloth or paper towel and once again with a dry towel to remove any sauce or liquid from the rim of the jar. Place the canning lid on the jar and twist the canning ring on until it's just-snug on the jar. Process in the water bath for 10 minutes. Carefully remove the jars from the water bath with the canning tongs and place jars on a towel for 12 hours without touching. Store in the refrigerator after breaking the seal.

NOTES

STRAWBERRY CHUTNEY

We love Jamaican jerk seasoning in our family. We grill jerk chicken, pork, ribs, and even tofu throughout the year. A condiment that greatly complements this spicy food is chutney. This sweet and savory condiment is the perfect addition to not only a variety of proteins, but also on top of cream cheese and crackers. My chef friend even suggested muddling the chutney in a mojito.

....

Yield: 1 pint

2 cups fresh, organic strawberries, stems removed

1 cup (about ½ of 1 whole) red onion, chopped

¼ cup raisins, red or golden

¼ cup dried apricots

1 tbsp. (about 1-inch piece) fresh ginger root, peeled

1 garlic clove

1 tbsp. raw honey

2 tsp. organic apple cider vinegar

½ tsp. kosher salt

Put all ingredients in a food processor and pulse until it reaches the consistency you desire. I like the raisins and apricots to retain chunkiness. Transfer mixture into a clean pint jar or other fermentation vessel. The chutney is full of flavor immediately, but as it ferments, the intensity of the onion will fade, and it turns into a delicious ferment.

If using a pint jar, use a canning jar lid and ring to tightly close the jar to keep the air out. Store at room temperature, ideally between 60 and 75°F. You must burp the jar daily or open the jar, stir up the mixture, and push down the chutney to allow built-up carbon dioxide to escape. Keep out of direct sunlight or wrap a dish towel around the jar to keep light out.

Ferment 2 to 4 days. I recommend taste testing it daily to see how the flavor changes during the fermentation process. Once fermentation is complete, store in an airtight glass jar and refrigerate for up to 2 weeks.

NOTES

SPICY SUGAR SNAP PEA PICKLES

These spicy veggies are a great addition to any dish that could use a little extra crunch and spice! Regular-mouth canning jars are recommended for this recipe, as their design helps keep the vegetables pushed down.

....

Yield: 2 pints

1–1½ lb. sugar snap peas
1 carrot, peeled, diced, or julienned
2 jalapeño peppers, sliced
4 garlic cloves, chopped

Brine:

2 cups (5 percent acidity) distilled white vinegar
1 cup water
2 tsp. canning salt

Wash the pea pods, trim the ends, and remove the stringy portion. Cut the pea pods into thirds, making bite-sized pieces. Mix together the chopped-up peas, carrots, jalapeños, and garlic.

In a medium sized, nonreactive saucepan, bring the brine ingredients to a boil and simmer for 3 minutes.

Pack the prepared jars full of the vegetables and use a funnel to safely transfer the brine into the jars. Leave ½" headspace. Wipe the rims of the jars with a dampened, clean, lint-free cloth or paper towel and again with a dry towel. Place the canning lid on the jar and twist the ring on until it's just-snug on the jar. Process in the water bath canner for 10 minutes. Carefully remove the jars from the water bath with the canning tongs and place the jars on a towel for 12 hours without touching.

Allow the flavors to meld for at least two weeks before opening. The longer they sit, the spicier they'll get. Store in the refrigerator after breaking the seal.

NOTES

SUGAR SNAP PEA PICKLES

Sugar snaps are abundant in the spring and early summer. Fermenting them is a great way to preserve them well into the wintertime. The peas keep their lovely crunch and can be eaten from the jar, enjoyed as a dill pickle replacement, or used to cook with.

....

Yield: 1 quart

1 lb. fresh sugar snap peas
4 garlic cloves, halved

Brine:

1 tbsp. kosher salt,
   dissolved in 2 cups
   water

Wash sugar snap peas and remove any bruised or flawed areas. Snap off or cut away the ends and stringy portion of the peas but keep the pods.

Pack a clean quart jar with the peas, fitting them in as tightly as possible. Add the garlic cloves between the pea pods. After the jar is packed, pour the brine over the peas, submerging them completely. Leave about 1½ inches of headspace to fit a weight. Cover the ferment with a cheese cloth or other breathable cover to keep dust and bugs from entering your ferment.

Check on the ferment daily to make sure the brine remains over the peas and that no mold or yeast forms. If the brine is low, press down the weight to bring the brine back over the ferment. This is an 8-day ferment. Once fermentation is complete, store in an airtight glass jar and refrigerate.

NOTES

DANDELION JELLY

Dandelions are considered by many to be a nuisance that takes over the yard. Surprisingly, there are many uses for dandelions and their greens in the kitchen! Wine and tea can be made with the blossoms; the blooms can also be battered and fried to make a quick appetizer. The greens can be added to salads, homemade pizza, or even made into a pesto. Whether you find dandelions in your yard or in an open field, please make sure they come from a pesticide-free and fertilizer-free area. I harvest them from my yard and my neighbors' yards—I've never had anyone turn me down when I show up and ask to pick their dandelions! The best time to pick dandelion flowers is during a nice and sunny part of the day. The flowers open big, and it's easier to remove the petals this way. Also, little kids are awesome helpers and are happy to make a game out of quick flower harvesting.

....

Yield: 2 (8 oz.) jars

1 cup (about 100 flowers) dandelion petals

1¾ cups water

1 cup honey or 2 cups organic or non-GMO sugar if you prefer a stiffer jelly

1½ tsp. lemon juice

Once you have collected the dandelions, wash them and remove their stems so that only the flower remains. The green base of the flower needs to be removed; the yellow petals will be saved for the jelly. The easiest way I found to remove the petals is to rip the base of the flower, open the flower up, pick out the yellow petals, and put them into a measuring cup. It is nearly impossible to not get some of the green portion mixed in with the petals because your fingers will become sticky. A little green mixed in will not affect the flavor, but do your best separate the two.

Next, in a medium sauce pan, add the dandelion petals to water and simmer for 10 minutes. Let the pan cool and transfer to a glass bowl and cover for the night. The dandelion mixture can be left at room temperature.

After the petals have soaked overnight, use a fine mesh strainer to separate the dandelion liquid from the petals. Use the back of a spoon to press the petals into the strainer to remove additional liquid from them. In a medium-sized, nonreactive saucepan, heat the dandelion liquid, honey or sugar, and lemon juice and bring to a boil. Follow the package directions for adding pectin. Once pectin has been added in, turn off the heat and begin the next step.

Ladle the hot jelly into warm prepared jars. Use a funnel to safely transfer the jelly, leaving ¼ inch of headspace. Wipe the rims of the jars with a dampened, clean, lint-free towel or paper towel and again with a dry towel. Place the canning lid on the jar and twist the ring until it is just-snug on the jar. Process in the water bath canner for 10 minutes. Carefully remove the jars from the water bath with the canning tongs and place the jars on a towel for 12 hours without touching. Refrigerate after breaking the seal.

1.

Remove the petals from the green base.

2.

Simmer and let cool overnight.

3.

Strain the petals from the liquid.

4.

DANDELION BUDS

These little flavor bombs can be used as a replacement for capers. The bud of the dandelion is a small, green, unopened bud that is often found very close to the ground within the leafy area of the dandelion plant. They pinch off very easily if you give them a little twist while pulling.

....

Yield: 1 pint

2 cups dandelion buds
2 cloves garlic, halved
½ small onion (optional)
2 sprigs fresh thyme
   (optional)

Brine:

½ tbsp. kosher salt dissolved
   in 1 cup water

Harvest 2 cups of dandelion buds and soak them in cold water for a few minutes, stirring them around with your hand to remove any dirt or bugs that may have hitched a ride in. Rinse and repeat this process until the buds are clean and the water runs clear. Remove stems and discard any buds that are semi-open and showing yellow petals. You only want to ferment the tightly closed little green buds.

Pack the buds, garlic, and optional ingredients into a prepared pint jar and cover with brine until the buds are completely submerged. Use a weight to hold the buds under the brine. Use a canning jar lid and ring to tightly close the jar to keep the air out. Store at room temperature, ideally between 60 and 75°F. Keep out of direct sunlight or wrap a dish towel around the jar to keep the sun out.

Be sure to check on the ferment daily and burp it to release the carbon dioxide that is created during fermentation. This is a 5-day ferment. Once fermentation is complete, store in an airtight glass jar and refrigerate.

NOTES

PICKLED FENNEL

When it comes to this pickle, it is best served over a fish entrée, mixed into a salad, or topped on a sandwich.

··················

Yield: 2 pints or 4 (8 oz.) half pints

1 fennel bulb, fronds removed, thinly sliced
½ yellow onion, thinly sliced
1 tsp. dried basil
2 tsp. whole black peppercorns
2 tsp. yellow mustard seeds

Brine:

2 cups (5 percent acidity) distilled white vinegar
1 cup water
1 tbsp. canning salt
2 tbsp. lemon juice

Wash fennel and cut away any bruised or damaged areas. Thinly slice the fennel and onion.

In a nonreactive pot, bring the brine ingredients to a boil, add the fennel and onion, bring back to a boil, and simmer for 3 minutes. Divide the basil, peppercorns, and mustard seeds between the prepared jars.

Ladle the hot fennel and onion mixture into the jars., using a funnel to safely transfer the mixture. Leave ¼ inch of headspace. Wipe the rims of the jars with a dampened, clean, lint-free cloth or paper towel and again with a dry towel. Place the canning lid on each jar and twist on the ring until it's just-snug on the jar. Process in the water bath for 10 minutes. Carefully remove the jars from the water bath with the canning tongs and place them on a towel for 12 hours without touching. Let the flavors of the pickled fennel meld for at least 2 weeks before opening. Refrigerate after breaking the seal.

NOTES

FENNEL AND RADISH SLAW

This lovely colored pink slaw was a total experiment that turned into a favorite side to many meals in our household. The flavors meld together wonderfully.

....

Yield: 1 quart

1 fennel bulb, fronds
  removed, sliced
2 unpeeled watermelon
  radishes, thickly julienned
2 stalks celery, chopped
2 unpeeled carrots, grated
½ onion, thinly sliced
1 tbsp. kosher salt

Scrub the veggies and remove the ends and any bruised or damaged skins. There isn't a *right* way to chop up these vegetables, but the aforementioned notes are the way I prefer to chop them.

In a large, nonreactive bowl, mix the salt with the prepared veggies and pack them into a glass jar or crock, pushing down the mixture with your hands or a tamping tool. Within an hour, the natural liquid from the vegetables should release enough brine to cover the vegetables. If there is not enough brine to cover the vegetables, mix extra brine (1 tbsp. dissolved in 2 cups water) and add it to the jar/crock until the vegetables are covered. Use a weight to hold the vegetables underneath the brine. Cover jar/crock with a cheese cloth or other breathable cover to keep dust and bugs from entering your ferment. Store at room temperature, ideally between 60 and 75°F. Keep out of direct sunlight or wrap a dish towel around the jar.

This is a 3-week ferment. Check on the ferment every few days to make sure the brine remains over the veggies and that no mold forms. If the brine is low, press down the weight to bring the brine back over the ferment. Once fermentation is complete, store in an airtight glass jar and refrigerate.

NOTES

FIDDLEHEAD FERN PICKLES

These unique-looking curly cuties are briefly available in the spring. I have seen them for sale at the farmers' market a few times over the years, and they were available at my local co-op this year (hooray!). They can be a bit hard to come by, but they are so delectable, which is why I encourage you to keep your eye out for them. They can be mail-ordered from the East Coast if you cannot find them in your area. Fiddleheads are not the same ferns that many have growing in their yards. In fact, some varieties found in our yards are toxic. Be sure that if you decide to forage for fiddleheads, you know exactly what you are looking for. Regular-mouth jars are recommended, as they're designed to help keep the fiddleheads packed together and pushed down.

In addition to being delicious when pickled, fiddlehead ferns are incredibly good sautéed with butter and garlic. I encourage you to buy extra to cook up after you've canned and fermented a couple of batches.

....

Yield: 4 pints

1 pound fiddlehead ferns (much will be discarded after trimming)
4 cloves garlic, sliced
2 tsp. dill seeds
2 tsp. yellow mustard seeds

Brine:

4 cups (5 percent acidity) distilled white vinegar
4 cups water
½ cup pickling salt

It is important to clean the fiddlehead ferns well and remove any of the brown, dry areas attached to the ferns. Cut off the ends and set aside any ferns that don't look green and fresh; you can cook those less-than-perfect ones later for a snack.

Once cleaned, fill up a pot or bowl with ice and cold water and let the fiddleheads soak for 1 hour. Strain and rinse with cold water.

Bring a medium pot of water to a boil and blanch the fiddlehead ferns. Wait for the water to begin to boil, then start the timer for 2 minutes. Drain and add the fiddleheads to an ice bath until cooled.

In a nonreactive pan, bring the brine ingredients to a boil for 5 minutes, then reduce heat to a low simmer.

Divide the garlic, dill seeds, and mustard seeds between the prepared jars. Pack the jars with fiddleheads as tightly as possible without bruising or damaging them. The fiddleheads will shrink up during the water bath process, so in order to avoid having a jar full of brine, be very intentional about packing the jar as well as you are able.

Ladle the hot brine over the fiddleheads. Use a funnel to safely transfer the brine into the jar, leaving ½ inch of headspace. Wipe the rims of the jars with a dampened, clean, lint-free cloth or paper towel and again with a dry towel. Place the canning lid on the jar and twist the canning ring on until it's just-snug on the jar. Process in the water bath for 10 minutes. Carefully remove the jars from the water bath with the canning tongs and place jars on a towel for 12 hours without touching.

Though the fiddleheads will have immediate flavor, they are best if they pickle for 4 weeks or more before opening. Refrigerate after breaking the seal.

NOTES

FIDDLEHEAD FERNS

Fiddlehead ferns have a bad rap for causing foodborne illness when consumed raw or undercooked. Though the process of fermentation does change the fiddlehead, I found it important to make note of this. According to the University of Maine, symptoms of eating raw or undercooked fiddleheads can include diarrhea, nausea, vomiting, abdominal cramps, and headaches generally within 30 minutes to 12 hours after consumption. That being said, a lot of people disagree that they have any harmful effect; they believe the illness could be caused by E. coli from the farm or other exterior nuisances. Please make sure they are properly cleaned before eating. Take this information and use your best judgement now knowing the risks. If you see it as too much of a risk, stick to canning them.

······················

Yield: I quart

½ pound fiddlehead ferns (much will be discarded after trimming)
2 garlic cloves, sliced
I bay leaf

Brine:

I ½ tbsp. kosher salt, dissolved in 3 cups water

It is important to clean the fiddlehead ferns well and remove any of the brown, dry areas that are attached to the ferns. Trim the ends.

Fill the jar with the garlic and bay leaf. Pack the jar with fiddleheads and leave room in the jar for a weight.

Add the brine to the jar until the fiddleheads are completely submerged. Add a clean weight to keep the brine over the fiddleheads.

Cover jar with a cheese cloth or other breathable cover to keep dust and bugs from entering your ferment. Store at room temperature, ideally between 60 and 75°F. Keep out of direct sunlight.

This is an 8-to-12-day ferment. Be sure to check on the ferment every few days to make sure the brine still remains over the fiddleheads and that no mold or yeast forms. If the brine is low, press down the weight to bring the brine back to the top of the ferment. Taste after 8 days to determine if the fiddlehead has a flavor sour enough to your liking. If not, allow to ferment a couple more days and taste again. Repeat until the desired flavor is reached. Once fermentation is complete, store in an airtight glass jar and refrigerate.

GARLIC SCAPE PICKLES

Because of their brief appearance in the spring, their great flavor, and my garlic addiction, I love having canned scapes on hand to use throughout the year. Pickled scapes are fabulous when added to a sandwich, cut up in a salad, or even tossed into a cocktail. Though I have not seen them in stores yet, I have seen them in abundance at farmers' markets around the states. Fresh garlic scapes are phenomenal when lightly oiled, salted, and grilled for a minute or so on each side. They make a unique and fun finger food for all ages to enjoy.

....

Yield: 2 pints

3 bundles thin scapes (thick ones tend to be chewy)

2 cloves garlic, sliced (optional)

2 tsp. yellow mustard seeds

Brine:

2 cups (5 percent acidity) distilled white vinegar

2 cups water

1 tbsp. canning salt

Wash the scapes and trim off the tough ends (typically, the bottom couple of inches). They tend to have a natural point of breakage, like asparagus. You can either leave the flower bloom on or trim it off; that is up to you. It will not affect the flavor one way or the other to leave the bloom on.

In a nonreactive pan, bring the brine ingredients to a boil, stirring until the salt is dissolved, then reduce heat to a low simmer. Divide the garlic and mustard seeds between the prepared jars.

To pack the jars, you can either chop up the scapes into pieces or do as shown in my photo and wrap them into circles. I think it gives the jar a very beautiful and unique look to wrap them in the jar. To do this, just wrap a few scapes at a time around your fingers and carefully place them in the jar.

Ladle the hot brine over the scapes. Use a funnel to safely transfer the brine into the jar, leaving ½ inch of headspace. Wipe the rims of the jars with a dampened, clean, lint-free cloth or paper towel and once again with a dry towel. Place the canning lid on and twist the canning ring on until it's just-snug on the jar. Process in the water bath for 10 minutes. Carefully remove the jars from the water bath with the canning tongs and place jars on a towel for 12 hours without touching. Allow scapes to pickle for 2 weeks before tasting. Store in the refrigerator after breaking the seal.

NOTES

GARLIC SCAPE PICKLES

Fermented scapes are great, but I feel like a little of the garlic flavor is lost during both fermentation and water bath canning, so I like to add extra garlic. As with pickled scapes, fermented scapes are great on sandwiches, in salads, or used as a cocktail garnish.

....

Yield: 1 quart

3 bundles thin scapes (thick ones tend to be chewy)

1 garlic clove, crushed (optional)

Brine:

1 tbsp. kosher salt, dissolved in 2 cups of water

Wash the scapes and trim off the tough ends; typically, the bottom couple of inches. They tend to have a natural point of breakage, like asparagus. You can either leave the flower bloom on or trim it off; that is up to you. It will not affect the flavor one way or the other to leave the bloom on.

To pack the jars, you can either chop up the scapes into pieces or do as shown in my photo and wrap them into circles. I think wrapping them up gives the jar a very beautiful and unique look. To do this, just wrap a few scapes at a time around your fingers and carefully place them in the jar. Cut up any extra scapes and shove them down the middle of the jar to pack it as much as possible.

Once the jar is packed, pour the brine over the scapes. Use a weight to hold the scapes underneath the brine. Cover the jar or crock with a cheese cloth or other breathable cover to keep dust and bugs from entering your ferment. Store at room temperature, ideally between 60 and 75°F. If you are using a clear jar, keep out of direct sunlight or wrap a dish towel around the jar to keep the light out.

This is a 2-week ferment. Check on the ferment every few days to make sure the brine remains over the scapes and that no mold or yeast forms. If the brine is low, press down the weight to bring the brine back over the ferment. Once fermentation is complete, store in an airtight glass jar and refrigerate.

Bonus Recipe: Garlic Scape Spread

Yield:

Parmesan cheese
Olive oil
Pepper

Purée canned or fermented scapes in a food processor with Parmesan cheese, olive oil, and pepper. Toss the mixture with pasta or zucchini noodles, and you will have a quick and delicious meal you'll dream about. It's also a flavor-packed spread for Italian-style sandwiches!

SPICY SPRING ONION RELISH

This zesty relish brings everything to life. Enjoy it as a chili topping, on eggs, over fish, or even on a burger. The opportunities are endless for this flavorful condiment! Spring onions are visually similar to scallions but are thicker and have a more bulbous white end. If you use scallions for this recipe instead of spring onions, you will likely need to double the number of scallions that you will need to use due to size difference.

....

Yield: 2 pints

4 bundles (about 12–16 stalks) spring onions
1 jalapeño, thinly sliced
½ tsp. celery seeds
½ tsp. mustard seeds

Brine:

2 cups (5 percent acidity) distilled white vinegar
2 cups water
¼ cup pickling salt

Clean the spring onions by cutting off the root and green ends and pealing back the thin outer layer; just the white portion of the onion is used in this recipe. Very finely slice the onions with a sharp knife or mandolin.

In a nonreactive pan, bring the brine ingredients to a boil, keep at a high simmer for 3 minutes, then reduce to a low simmer.

Mix onions, jalapeños, and celery and mustard seeds in a bowl and evenly mix the ingredients. Pack two jars with the onion mixture. Press the onions down firmly in each jar without smashing them. Try and pack as much as you can into each pint; lightly filled jars will result in a jar full of brine.

Ladle the hot brine over the onion mix. Use a funnel to safely transfer the brine into the jar, leaving ½ inch of headspace. Wipe the rims of the jars with a dampened, clean, lint-free cloth or paper towel and once again with a dry towel. Place the canning lid on the jar and twist the canning ring on until it fits just-snug. Process in the water bath for 10 minutes. Carefully remove the jars from the water bath with the canning tongs and place jars on a towel for 12 hours without touching. Allow flavors to meld for at least 2 weeks before tasting. Store in the refrigerator after breaking the seal.

SPRING ONION KIMCHI

Kimchi is by far one of my favorite things in the world to eat and has been since I was just a toddler. I was blessed to grow up in a home that often had it on hand. These fermented spring onions can be eaten as a snack, added to any meal as a side dish, or eaten over a bowl of rice.

....

Yield: 1 quart

4 bunches (about 35 stalks) spring onions
2 tbsp. kosher salt
4 cloves garlic
1-inch piece fresh ginger, skin removed
1 tbsp. Red Boat fish sauce or other fish sauce without MSG and preservatives (optional)
½ cup coarse hot pepper flakes

Wash spring onions, cut away the roots, the outer thin layer, and any old or damaged-looking green portions around the onions. When onions are clean and prepped, rinse again with cold water.

Place onions in a glass dish such as a Pyrex brand 9 x 13-inch baking dish. Sprinkle salt over onions. Use hands to mix salt evenly around onions and let sit for 2 hours. Mix onions after 1 hour. After 2 hours, rinse the salt away with cold water and let drain in a colander.

In a food processor, add garlic, ginger, and fish sauce and pulse until puréed. Transfer the mixture into a medium bowl and add hot pepper flakes. Mix well.

In another large glass dish such as a Pyrex brand 9 x 13-inch baking dish, add the rinsed onions and pepper mixture. Coat the spring onions thoroughly with the mixture. Cut onions into 2-inch chunks and mix again. Transfer the onions smothered in the kimchi base into a clean jar or other fermenting vessel of choice. Pack the onions in well, but leave about 1 inch of space from the onions to the rim of the jar.

Cover each jar or crock with a cheese cloth or other breathable cover to keep dust and bugs from entering your ferment. Store at room temperature, ideally between 60 and 75°F. If you are using a clear jar, keep out of direct sunlight.

Ferment at room temperature for 2 days and transfer to an airtight container. Store in the refrigerator for 2 weeks before eating. The onion mixture will continue to slowly ferment in the cool fridge.

NAPA CABBAGE KIMCHI

The kimchi base of this recipe can be applied to cucumbers or green beans to make other variations of delicious kimchi.

· · · · · · · · · · · · · · · · · · · ·

Yield: 3 quarts

2 heads Napa cabbage

¼ cup kosher salt

6 cloves garlic

2-inch piece ginger or more if desired, peeled

1 medium onion

1–2 tbsp. Red Boat fish sauce or other fish sauce without MSG and preservatives (optional)

1 cup coarse hot pepper powder (for a spicier kimchi, mix 1 tbsp. of cayenne pepper into the hot pepper powder)

5 green onions, cut into 1-inch pieces

Wash the cabbage well between each leaf. Cut each cabbage in half lengthwise and rinse again with cold water. Cut slits into the core of the cabbage so that the salt can penetrate and soften the hard core. Sprinkle salt in between each leaf and gently massage the salt into each leaf. The salt not only gives the cabbage flavor, but also tenderizes it. Once the cabbage is evenly salted, allow the cabbage to sit for 4 hours as the cabbage shrinks and the natural brine is created.

Use a food processor to purée the garlic, ginger, onion, and fish sauce together. Add this mixture to a bowl and add in the coarse pepper powder. Combine ingredients and mix well. Clean the green onions by removing the root ends and the thin outer layer of the onion. Cut onions into 1-inch pieces and add to the hot pepper mixture. Stir ingredients together. After 4 hours of salting the cabbage, add the hot pepper kimchi mixture to the cabbage and mix well, coating every cabbage piece. Transfer kimchi into clean quart jars or another fermentation vessel of choice and leave 2 inches of headspace so the jars do not overflow during fermentation. If using a canning jar, tightly twist on the canning lid and ring to keep the air out. You must burp the jars daily or open the jar, push down the kimchi, and allow any excess carbon dioxide to escape.

I recommend taste testing daily to see how the flavor changes during the fermentation process. (I can't help but eat some kimchi immediately after putting it together.) I personally think the flavor is best on day 3, but I normally let it ferment the full 7 days. Store at room temperature, ideally between 60 and 75°F. If you are using a clear jar, keep out of direct sunlight or wrap a towel around the jar to keep the light out. This is a 5–7-day ferment. Store in airtight containers and refrigerate once fermentation is complete.

SUMMER

SPICY PICKLED CARROTS

These carrot pickles retain a nice crunch after processing. Cut them into spears, round coins, or use a crinkle cutter if you prefer; in the end, they will all end up with the same great flavor.

....

Yield: 3 pints

1 lb. carrots
6 garlic cloves, sliced
3 tsp. yellow mustard seeds
3 tbsp. red pepper flakes or
   hot peppers, sliced

Brine:

2 cups (5 percent acidity)
   distilled white vinegar
2 cups water
¼ cup pickling salt

Clean the carrots, trim off the ends, and peel them. It is preferable to use thin or medium-sized carrots when making carrot pickles. If you only have large carrots available, halve and/or quarter them lengthwise. Cut them to fit in the jar, which is about 4 inches if you are using pint jars. Consider using a colorful variety of carrots to liven up the look of the jars.

In a nonreactive pan, bring the brine ingredients to a boil, keep at a high simmer 3 minutes, then reduce to a low simmer. Divide the garlic, mustard seeds, and pepper flakes or hot peppers between the jars. Pack the jars with carrots.

Ladle the hot brine over the carrots. Use a funnel to safely transfer the brine into each jar, leaving ½ inch of headspace. Wipe the rims of the jars with a dampened, clean, lint-free cloth or paper towel and again with a dry towel. Place the canning jar lid on each jar and twist on the canning ring until it fits just-snug. Process in the water bath for 10 minutes. Carefully remove the jars from the water bath with the canning tongs and place jars on a towel for 12 hours without touching. Allow the carrots to pickle for 4 weeks before tasting. Store in the refrigerator after breaking the seal.

NOTES

GARLICKY CARROT PICKLES

These garlicky carrots taste great as a snack, a side dish, cut up or shredded into salads, and, of course, in a Bloody Mary. From my experience, fermented carrots frequently get kham yeast. This is common with high-sugar vegetables, so be attentive to this during the fermentation process. If you see any yeast growing, use a paper towel to carefully dab it out of the brine.

....

Yield: I quart

I lb. carrots
4 cloves garlic, crushed
Optional: to make this
   ferment spicy, add
   I halved jalapeño
   or other spicy
   pepper and pack
   into each jar

Brine:

I tbsp. kosher salt
   dissolved in 2 cups
   water

Wash carrots and trim off the ends. No need to peel; the skin on the carrots will aid in the fermentation process. Cut the carrots to fit in the jar. Remember to leave 2 inches of room for the brine and weight, and space for the carrots to ferment. It is preferable to use thin to medium-sized carrots for this recipe. If you only have large carrots available to you, you'll need to halve and/or quarter them lengthwise. Consider using a colorful variety of carrots to liven up the aesthetic of the jar. If you include cosmic carrots, the brine will turn a pretty pink color at the end of the fermentation process.

Pack the jar with the carrots, carefully fitting them in as snug as possible. Add the garlic between the carrots. Once the jar is packed, pour the brine over the carrots until they are covered by about ½ to 1 inch of brine.

Use a weight to hold the vegetables underneath the brine. Cover jar/crock with a cheese cloth or other breathable cover to keep dust and bugs from entering the ferment. Store at room temperature, ideally between 60 and 75°F. If using a clear jar, keep out of direct sunlight or wrap a dish towel around the jar.

This is a 10-day ferment. Be sure to check on the ferment every couple of days to make sure the brine remains over the carrots and that no mold or yeast forms. Once fermentation is complete, store in an airtight glass jar and refrigerate.

Recipe Variation: Carrot Pickles with Pickling Spice

Brine:

I ½ tbsp. kosher salt
   dissolved in 3 cups
   water

Add 1 tbsp. of premixed pickling spices to the bottom of the jar before packing it with carrots and adding brine. It will create a pickled carrot perfect for fall. The flavors of allspice, clove, coriander, cinnamon, and ginger all shine, making this pickle a pleasant surprise on a holiday relish tray.

CARROTS WITH LEEK AND THYME

This recipe was developed by Kylene and Mel Guse, sisters and owners of Gyst Fermentation Bar in Minneapolis, Minnesota.

"We love these fermented carrots. They are crunchy, refreshing, and delicious. Use them in fresh salads or as an accoutrement to a beautiful cheese board, or as a crunchy, healthy snack!" —Ky

....

Yield: 1 quart

1 lb. carrots, skin on, cut into medallions
½ leek, thinly cut
2 tsp. thyme (add more, or less, to your liking)
1 tbsp. kosher salt

In a large glass or other nonreactive bowl, mix the carrots and leek together. In a separate, smaller bowl, mix thyme and salt together.

Add the thyme/salt mixture to the carrots and leeks, mixing well with your hands. Let the mixture sit for 1 to 2 hours as the natural brine is created.

Transfer the mixture and brine into a quart jar or other vessel. Use a weight to push the vegetables under the brine. Cover with a breathable top. Store in a cool place and ferment to your liking.

NOTES

PICKLED JALAPEÑO SLICES

I'm just going to go ahead and tell you to triple this recipe right now. If you like pickled peppers, you will blow through 4 pints in a couple of weeks. I make more and more each year, and it's never enough. These are one of the most requested preserves that I make.

·····················

Yield: 4 pints

8 cloves of garlic, halved

4 tsp. mustard seeds

4 tsp. dill seeds

2 lb. jalapeños, stems removed, sliced

Brine:

3 cups (5 percent) distilled white vinegar

3 cups water

3 tbsp. pickling salt

In a nonreactive pan, bring the brine ingredients to a boil, reduce heat to a simmer for 3 minutes, stir until the salt is dissolved, then reduce heat to a low simmer.

Divide the garlic, mustard seeds, and dill seeds between the jars. Pack the jars with the jalapeño slices. Push them down carefully without damaging the slices. You must make sure to push down the slices as you pack the jars; otherwise, you'll end up with a jar full of brine and only half full of jalapeños. Ladle the hot brine over the jalapeños. Use a funnel to safely transfer the brine into the jar, leaving ½ inch of headspace. Use a stainless-steel butter knife or other similar tool to get rid of any air bubbles trapped in the jar. Wipe the rims of the jars with a dampened, clean, lint-free cloth and again with a dry cloth and place the canning the lid on. Twist the canning ring on until it's just-snug on the jar. Process in the water bath for 10 minutes. Carefully remove the jars from the water bath with the canning tongs and place jars on a towel for 12 hours without touching.

Though the jalapeños will be good immediately after making, I recommend letting them pickle for 2 weeks before tasting; that will give the flavors a chance to meld together. Store in the refrigerator after breaking the seal.

Recipe Variation: Refrigerator Pickle

Water bath sealing the jalapeños will cause them to lose their crispness. If you want the crunch of the jalapeño to remain, follow all the directions up until the water bath part. Fill the jars with jalapeños, add the brine, wipe the rims, add the lid and ring, but do not water bath seal. Skip to the step of putting the jars on a towel to let them cool. Once cooled, they need to be refrigerated. The jalapeños will not be shelf-stable, but they will be flavorful and crunchy.

Recipe Variation: Pickled Eggs

Once the jar of jalapeño slices is almost empty and has only a few jalapeños, spices, and garlic pieces left, fill it with peeled, hard-boiled eggs. Let the eggs pickle in the brine for at least 2 weeks, refrigerated. This brine makes the most delicious pickled egg I've ever had. My friends agree—the longer it pickles, the tastier it gets! About 10 hard-boiled eggs fit into a quart jar.

JALAPEÑO SAUCE

This particular recipe uses jalapeño peppers, but the basic guidelines can be applied to any hot pepper of your choosing. I like to purchase mixed peppers from the farmers' market and turn that into a hot sauce—those have turned out to be my favorites! I prefer to use a glass jar with an airlock when fermenting this recipe. Jalapeños are prone to kahm yeast, and I do not get that when using an airlock. If you do not own an airlock system, be adamant about checking in on your ferment daily to catch any unwanted yeast that may begin growing.

....

Yield: 1 pint finished hot sauce

4 cups jalapeño peppers
10 garlic cloves, halved

Brine:

1½ tbsp. kosher salt dissolved in 3 cups water

Wash the jalapeños, remove the stems and any other flawed areas, and cut the peppers in half lengthwise. Pack a quart jar tightly with hot peppers, mixing the garlic in with the peppers.

Pour the brine over the jalapeños, submerging them completely. Use a weight to push the pepper slices and garlic under the brine. Store at room temperature, ideally between 60 and 75°F. If you are fermenting in a clear jar, wrap a dish towel around the jar to keep the sunlight out.

Ferment for 3 weeks. At the 3-week mark, I recommend smelling the ferment and even tasting a small sample of the brine. If it tastes good and has spice, I feel comfortable moving to step two of this process. If the brine doesn't have much flavor, let it ferment for another week and taste the brine again. Keep doing this until the brine is full of flavor.

Once you are ready to turn the fermented peppers into hot sauce, you must drain the brine from the peppers and garlic. Pour the brine into a measuring cup and set aside. Put the hot peppers and garlic into a food processor with a quarter cup of brine and purée it. If the peppers aren't puréeing well in the mixer, add a little more brine to get things moving. Keep adding brine until the sauce is completely puréed.

For the next step, take a small fine-mesh strainer and set it on a large measuring cup. Pour the pepper purée in the mesh strainer and let the liquid drip into the measuring cup. Use the back of a spoon to push the purée into the strainer; get as much liquid out of the pepper purée as you can.

The drained liquid is your hot sauce. Once all liquid is collected, transfer the hot sauce to a clean airtight glass container or jar and refrigerate.

JALEPEÑO SAUCE: STEP-BY-STEP

1.

Once peppers are fermented and ready for Step 2, drain the peppers and garlic from the brine, reserve the brine, and set aside.

2.

Purée and strain.

3.

Transfer hot pepper liquid into a clean, airtight glass container and refrigerate. Enjoy!

THE PERFECT GARLIC DILL PICKLE

It took me years of experimenting with loads of different ingredients to figure out the perfect dill pickle recipe. It turns out the simplest recipe is the best. I use this brine for almost all of my various pickled veggies now because it's easy and it tastes phenomenal. A lot of canners are intimidated by making pickles because the end result is mushy. I have never made a soft pickle in all my years of canning, and if you follow my directions closely, you won't, either.

....

Yield: 5–6 quarts

¼ bushel small pickling cucumbers

2 bulbs garlic, halved

6 tsp. dill seeds or 1 sprig fresh dill

6 tsp. mustard seeds

Optional: 1-2 jalapeños, quartered, or 1 halved habanero peppers for extra spice

Brine:

8 cups (5 percent acidity) distilled white vinegar

8 cups water

3/4 cup canning salt

I recommend using small pickling cucumbers for this recipe. In order to get small pickling cucumbers from the farmers' market, you should go to the market as soon as it opens because they are often in high demand and sell out quickly. The ideal size is a 3-inch or smaller pickling cucumber, which will allow you to pack the jar with two levels of cukes. I believe that the small size also contributes to the crunchiness of the canned pickle. Always ask the farmer when the cucumbers were harvested. You want ones that were picked the day of or the night before. Feel the cucumbers and make sure they feel firm and look fresh. Always plan to preserve the pickles the same day you buy them. Freshness is a key contributor for crunchy dills.

I keep a 5-gallon food-grade bucket aside for pickle making. Fill the bucket with cucumbers and use the garden hose to fill up the bucket with water. Carefully swish the cucumbers around in the water and rinse off any flower blooms or dirt. Repeat this step until the water runs clear. Then, fill the bucket with fresh water and a lot of ice, giving the cucumbers an ice bath for 1 hour.

While the cucumbers are in the ice bath, prep the garlic.

Wash each cucumber by hand. Using a vegetable brush, scrub off dirt and discard any bruised cucumbers that don't look up to par. Once all are scrubbed, rinse them again with cold water and strain them.

Once the pickles are clean, trim off both ends and any flawed areas. Do not use any mushy or damaged cucumbers.

In a large nonreactive pot, bring the brine ingredients to a boil and simmer for 5 minutes, then reduce heat to a low simmer. Divide the garlic, dill seeds, and mustard seeds between the jars. Carefully pack the pickles on end, fitting them in as if you were doing a Tetris puzzle. You want the jar packed well and to be tightly filled with cucumbers. Cut larger cucumbers in half if need be and fit them in as needed. If making spicy pickles, add jalapeños in with the cucumbers when packing the jars.

Ladle the hot brine into the jars. Use a funnel to safely transfer the brine into each jar, leaving ½ inch of headspace. Use a stainless-steel butter knife or other nonreactive tool to get rid of any air bubbles trapped in the jar. Wipe the rims of the jars with a dampened, clean, lint-free cloth or paper towel and then again with a dry towel. Place the canning jar lid on the jar and twist on the ring until it's just-snug on the jar. Process in the water bath for 10 minutes. Carefully remove the jars from the water bath with the canning tongs and place jars on a towel for 12 hours without touching.

I recommend letting these pickle for 2 months or more before tasting, as that will give the flavors a chance to meld together. Store in the refrigerator after breaking the seal.

NOTES

THE PERFECT GARLIC DILL PICKLE: STEP-BY-STEP

1.

2.

Rinse cucumbers in a 5-gallon food-grade bucket until the water runs clear. Gently swish the cucumbers around with your hand to loosen any dirt or flower buds.

Place the pickling cucumbers in an ice bath for at least 1 hour.

3.

4.

Wash each cucumber.

Trim off the ends and any flawed areas.

5.

Cut larger cucumbers in half if need be.

6.

If making spicy pickles, quarter jalepeños or halve habanero peppers.

7.

Divide garlic, mustard seeds, and dill seeds between the jars.

8.

Carefully pack the jar with cucumbers.

9.

Ladle hot brine into the jars.

10.

PICKLES

When I think of fermented pickles, I think of thick, garlicky, big pickles, which is quite the opposite of what I use when I make canned pickles. Conveniently, larger pickling cucumbers are more readily available at farmers' markets during the summer. I prefer to use my glass jar with an airlock or a fermentation crock with a water seal when making pickles. The recipe will vary depending on the size of your fermentation vessel, so adjust accordingly. The leaves are crucial to making crunchy fermented pickles because of their naturally occurring tannins. The pickles will have great flavor without the leaves, but they will be soft. A tip for always having leaves on hand is to freeze them.

....

Yield: 1.5L Fermentation Vessel (or 1-2 quarts if using Mason-style canning jars)

1–2 lb. (4½–5 inch) pickling cucumbers

10–15 garlic cloves or more if desired, halved

2 tbsp. dill seeds or 1 sprig fresh dill

1 tbsp. yellow mustard seeds

3–5 grape leaves, oak leaves, or raspberry leaves

3 jalapeños, sliced (optional, for spice)

Brine:

2 tbsp. kosher salt, dissolved in 4 cups water

Wash the pickles and let them sit in cold ice water for up to 1 hour, then strain. Put the cucumbers, garlic, dill seeds, mustard seeds, optional jalapeños, and leaves in a clean jar, crock, or other fermentation vessel. Pour the brine over the cucumbers and use a weight to keep the vegetables submerged.

If using an airlock system, set up the airlock on the fermentation vessel. If using a crock with a water seal, pour water in the seal and make sure the lid is sealed all the way around. If using a canning jar, cover the jar with a cheese cloth or other breathable cover to keep dust and bugs from entering.

Store at room temperature, ideally between 60 and 75°F. If using a clear glass jar, cover with a dish towel to keep the sunlight out. Check on the ferment every few days to make sure the brine remains over the cucumbers and more often if you are not using an airtight vessel.

This is a 30-day or more ferment. The brine will turn cloudy and sediment will likely begin to show up at the bottom of the ferment or on the pickles. This is a normal part of the fermentation process and a sign that things are progressing as they should. Once the pickles are done fermenting, transfer them to an airtight jar and refrigerate.

POLISH DILL PICKLES

Kryz and Emily Kociolek are the owners of Stone Creek Trading in Illinois. I use many of their crocks and supplies when fermenting. They have so graciously shared their family's Polish pickle recipe.

"Kryz grew up in Poland and remembers always seeing crocks of bubbly ferments in the basement of everyone's house. This is a recipe developed by Kryz's father, who makes the best pickles!" —Emily

....

Yield: 5L Fermentation Crock (for smaller yield, adjust recipe accordingly)

5–6 lb. small cucumbers
6 cloves garlic, sliced
⅓ bunch fresh dill
1 tbsp. yellow mustard seeds
1 tsp. whole allspice
1 tbsp. fresh horseradish root, sliced
1–3 grape leaves (optional)

Brine:

6 tbsp. kosher salt dissolved in 3 quarts water

Wash the cucumbers and poke a few holes at both ends with a knife or fork. Place cucumbers in the crock, mixing in the garlic, dill, mustard seeds, allspice, horseradish root, and optional grape leaves. Use weights to hold the pickles down and pour the brine over the cucumbers until it covers the weights.

Ferment for 3 to 4 days at room temperature and then move to a cooler place. Pickles can be eaten at any point during the fermentation process. When desired sourness is reached, transfer pickles and brine to an airtight glass container and refrigerate.

NOTES

SRIRACHA GARLIC CLOVES

These pickled garlic cloves are sweet and spicy. Add them to a cheese platter, purée them with some brine and mix with softened cream cheese for a flavorful dip, or chop up fresh parsley, mix with goat cheese and the puréed garlic, and serve on a toasted baguette—YUM!

....

Yield: I (8 oz.) jar

1–2 (¾ cup) garlic bulbs
½ cup red bell peppers, diced

Brine:

½ cup (5 percent acidity) distilled white vinegar
I tsp. pickling salt
2 tbsp. Sriracha sauce

Peel garlic and rinse with cold water. Cut large cloves in half. In a nonreactive saucepan, bring the brine ingredients to a boil and simmer for 3 minutes. Mix the garlic and red bell peppers together in a bowl and transfer them to a prepared canning jar. Pack the garlic and bell peppers in well without bruising the cloves.

Ladle the hot brine over the garlic. Use a funnel to safely transfer the brine into the jar, leaving ¼ inch of headspace. Wipe the rim of the jar with a dampened, clean, lint-free cloth or paper towel and again with a dry towel. Place the canning lid on the jar and twist on the canning ring until it's just-snug on the jar. Process in the water bath canner for 10 minutes. Carefully remove the jars from the water bath with canning tongs and place the jars on a towel for 12 hours without touching. Let the mixture pickle for 4 weeks before opening. Refrigerate after breaking the seal.

NOTES

GARLIC SPREAD

This spread makes pretty much everything taste better. Organically grown garlic is preferred for this recipe (and any fermented recipe) because of a controversy regarding nonorganic garlic being bleached and chemically treated to kill off bugs and other pests. If this is the case, your inorganically grown garlic will not ferment properly.

· · · · · · · · · · · · · · · · · · ·

Yield: 1 half pint

3 bulbs garlic, peeled

1 tsp. kosher salt

Peel garlic, rinse with cold water, and dry. Place garlic in a food processor and process until it is broken down into a spreadable consistency. Transfer the garlic spread into a clean half-pint jar and mix in the salt. Stir well. Use a canning jar lid and ring to tightly screw the lid on and keep the air out. Daily burping of the ferment is required to release any carbon dioxide that is created during fermentation. When checking on the ferment, remove the lid, stir up the mixture, pack it back down in the jar, and screw the lid on tightly. Store at room temperature, ideally between 60 and 75°F. If fermenting in a clear jar, wrap a dish towel around the jar to keep the sunlight out.

This is a 30-day ferment. Once fermentation is complete, store in an airtight glass container and refrigerate.

Recipe Variation: Garlic Cloves Fermented in Honey

One recipe that I continue to see all over is garlic fermented in honey. The garlic infuses the honey for an incredible garlicky-flavored honey that is great to cook with, or to make into salad dressings. The garlic cloves become mild and are great immune boosters when you're feeling under the weather. It's super easy to make and highly addictive.

Fill a clean jar or other fermentation vessel with peeled organic garlic cloves, leaving 1 to 2 inches of headspace. Cover the cloves with raw honey (locally grown honey if available). Use an airlock system or tightly cover the ferment with a canning jar lid and ring. If using a jar lid, you must burp the ferment daily and sometimes multiple times a day to release the carbon dioxide that is created during fermentation. Store at room temperature, ideally between 60 and 75°F. If fermenting in a clear jar, wrap a dish towel around the jar to keep the sunlight out. Ferment for 2 to 4 weeks. You can start eating it immediately, but the flavors change immensely during fermentation.

Recipe Variation: Garlic Cloves

After fermentation, these garlic cloves can be eaten straight from the jar or used as you would any regular clove of garlic.

....

Yield: 1 half pint

1–2 (¾ cup) garlic bulbs

Brine:

1 tsp. kosher salt dissolved in ¼ cup water

Peel the garlic, rinse with cold water, and transfer to a clean half-pint glass jar or other fermentation vessel of choice.

Pour brine over the garlic cloves until they are completely submerged. Leave 1 inch of headspace.

Use a canning jar lid and ring to tightly screw the lid on and keep the air out. Daily burping of the ferment is required to release any carbon dioxide that is created during fermentation. Store at room temperature, ideally between 60 and 75°F. If fermenting in a clear jar, wrap a dish towel around the jar to keep the sunlight out. This is a 30-day ferment. Once fermentation is complete, store in an airtight glass container and refrigerate.

NOTES

GRANDPA'S HOMEMADE SPAGHETTI SAUCE

My grandpa's spaghetti has been a favorite meal of mine and most of my family's for as long as I can remember. It was always a treat when spaghetti was served for dinner. Unfortunately, my grandpa has suffered from Parkinson's Disease for over twenty years and had to stop making the sauce himself. I was fortunate enough to learn the recipe by making the sauce with him back in my twenties, and it's one I will cherish for the rest of my life. My grandpa originally adapted the recipe from his aunt, and I have adapted his recipe to a water bath canner recipe.

....

Yield: 5–7 quarts

¼ bushel (about 25 lb.) tomatoes

1 tbsp. olive oil

1 medium onion, finely chopped

2 garlic cloves, minced

2 bay leaves

2 tbsp. garlic powder

1 tsp. parsley flakes

1 tsp. Italian seasoning

1 tsp. dried oregano

1 tsp. dried basil

1 tsp. dried summer savory

1 tsp. dried tarragon

1 tsp. white pepper

1 tbsp. salt

1 tsp. onion powder

2 tbsp. sugar

2 tbsp. lemon juice per jar

Wash tomatoes and cut off any bruised or damaged areas. Blanch the tomatoes. This process is easily done in stages and requires a large pot of boiling water and another pot or bowl of ice water. Bring a pot of water to a boil and add in tomatoes and once the pot begins to boil. Set the timer for 1 minute. Use a slotted spoon to carefully remove the tomatoes from the hot water and put them in the ice bath. You should see the tomato skins split while in the boiling water or once added to the ice bath. Repeat this process until all the tomatoes are blanched. This method will make removing the skins from the tomatoes a quick job, as the skin will easily fall off the fruit with a little rub of the fingers. Then, core the tomatoes and cut them into quarters.

Once all tomatoes are blanched, peeled, cored, and cut, add them to a large (at least 7 quarts) pot. Using a hand blender, break down the tomatoes into the consistency you want your sauce to have. I like to have a little chunkiness to my sauce. You can also break down the tomatoes using a food processor, but I've found the hand mixer is the easiest and least messy option.

In a medium frying pan, heat the olive oil and sauté the onion and garlic. Once the onion is translucent, it's done; this typically takes about 5 minutes. Add mixture to the tomatoes and add in all the seasonings. Mix well and heat the pot to a medium-high simmer. The sauce will need to cook for 2 to 3 hours to thicken. It must be stirred occasionally to avoid burning. Taste the sauce to determine if you want to add additional seasonings.

Once the sauce has thickened, remove the bay leaves. Prepare the quart jars with 2 tbsp. of lemon juice per jar. This will add acidity to the sauce that will keep it from growing unsafe bacteria.

Ladle the sauce into warm, prepared jars. Use a funnel to safely transfer the sauce, leaving ½ inch of headspace. Wipe the rims of the jars with a dampened, clean, lint-free cloth or paper towel and again with a dry towel. Place canning lid on the jar and twist the canning ring on until it's just-snug on the jar. Process in the water bath for 40 minutes. Carefully remove jars from the water bath with canning tongs and place the jars on a towel for 12 to 24 hours without touching. Refrigerate after breaking the seal.

Meat can be added to the sauce when served but not before, as a pressure canner would be required to preserve a recipe with meat. Italian sausage, meatballs, and mushrooms are perfect additions for this sauce when served, as well as a little fresh grated Parmesan cheese. My grandpa's spaghetti sauce also includes his homemade spice mix, which is not included in this recipe. But if you are a fan of spice, consider adding some crushed red pepper flakes, cayenne pepper, or diced jalapeños to the sauce.

NOTES

SPAGHETTI SAUCE: STEP-BY-STEP

1.

After boiling the tomatoes, place them in an ice bath.

2.

Once cooled, remove the skins from the tomatoes.

3.

Core tomatoes and cut them into quarters.

4.

Break down tomatoes to the consistency you desire. Add in sautéed onions and garlic.

5.

Add seasonings and simmer for 2 to 3 hours.

6.

CHERRY TOMATOES
WITH GARLIC AND FRESH BASIL

These appetizing tomatoes taste incredible just hours after putting the ingredients together but get even more intense after a few days of fermentation. I prefer to use a mixed variety of cherry tomatoes, but whatever you are growing in the garden or have on hand will work just fine. I like to eat them straight from the jar, but they are a beautiful addition to pasta, salads, kebab skewers, or a Bloody Mary.

....

Yield: I quart

3½ cups cherry tomatoes, any variety
5 fresh basil leaves
2 cloves garlic, chopped

Brine:

I tbsp. kosher salt dissolved in 2 cups water

Wash tomatoes and basil with cold water. Put the basil and chopped garlic at the bottom of the jar and fill the rest of the jar with cherry tomatoes, leaving at least 1 inch of space at the top.

Pour the brine over the tomatoes, completely submerging them. I don't use a weight for this ferment. I normally put a jar lid with ring over, airtight, instead of a cheese cloth. Either option will work, but if you tighten a lid and ring on this ferment, be sure to open the jar at least twice a day to burp it.

I encourage you to taste these a few hours after they are made, again 24 hours later, again 48 hours later, etc., to determine which taste you prefer the most. Ferment for up to 3 days at room temperature, ideally between 60 and 75°F. Once fermentation is complete, store in an airtight glass jar and refrigerate. The tomatoes tend to get softer the longer they ferment. I prefer to eat them within a couple of weeks.

NOTES

GRANDMA'S PICKLED BEETS

Grandma's favorite canned good.

·····················

Yield: about 4 quarts

8 lb. freshly harvested
  beets, small are preferred
  because they are more
  tender

Brine:

4 cups (5 percent acidity)
  distilled white vinegar
2 cups water
2 tsp. canning salt
2 cups organic or non-GMO
  sugar
2 tsp. ground cloves

Use a vegetable brush to gently scrub the beets clean. Trim off the leafy ends, place the beets in a pot of water, and bring it to a boil. Cook the beets until they are tender and easily pierced with a fork, about 25 minutes. Remove from heat, drain, and let cool.

Once cooled enough to handle, trim off the root-end of each beet and use your hands to break the outer layer of the skin. Use your thumbs to rub away the skin. Removing the skin can become a messy job. I recommend having a bowl for the discarded skins and another dish for the peeled beets. I normally do this over a large cutting board. It will look as if something dyed your hands bright pink, but it easily washes off with a little soapy water.

Slice beets to your desired size. I prefer to cut my beets into chunks, but you may prefer your beets sliced. Pack the beets into prepared canning jars.

In a large nonreactive pot, heat the brine ingredients and boil for 5 minutes, then reduce the heat to a low simmer. Ladle the hot brine over the beets. Use a funnel to safely transfer the brine into the jar, leaving ½ inch of headspace. Wipe the rims of the jars with a dampened, clean, lint-free cloth or paper towel and then again with a dry towel. Place the canning lid on the jar and twist the canning ring on until it's just-snug on the jar. Process in the water bath canner for 30 minutes. Carefully remove the jars from the water bath with the canning tongs and place the jars on a towel for 12 to 24 hours without touching. Store in the refrigerator after breaking the seal.

Recipe Variation: Purple Pickled Eggs

When the jar of pickled beets gets low, use the brine to pickle peeled, hard-boiled eggs. Within a few days, the brine will begin to turn the white portion of the egg purple. The longer the eggs pickle, the more the purple brine will penetrate, eventually coloring even the yolk. These purple eggs are especially a hit when turned into colorful deviled eggs! About 10 peeled, hard-boiled eggs fit into a quart-sized jar.

PICKLED BEETS

After fermentation, the beets will become more tender but will retain a nice crunchiness.

....

Yield: 1 quart

6 small beets

2 whole star anises

Brine:

1 tbsp. kosher salt,
   dissolved in 2 cups water

Gently scrub beets clean of any dirt but do not peel. Trim the ends off and uniformly cut the beets into ½-inch chunks. Pack beets into a small crock or jar and cover with brine until they are completely submerged. Use a weight to hold the beets underneath the brine.

Cover jar/crock with a cheese cloth or other breathable cover to keep dust and bugs from entering your ferment. Store at room temperature, ideally between 60 and 75°F. If you are using a clear jar, keep out of direct sunlight or wrap a dish towel around the jar to keep the light out.

This is a 2-week ferment. Be sure to check on the ferment every few days to make sure the brine remains over the beets and that no mold or yeast forms. If the brine is low, press the weight down to bring the brine back over the ferment. Once fermentation is complete, store in an airtight glass jar and refrigerate.

NOTES

BEET KVASS

This recipe was created by fermentation fanatic Jeremy Ogusky, owner of Ogusky Ceramics. He makes the gorgeous pottery crocks pictured throughout the book. He's also founder of the Boston Fermentation Festival! "Beet kvass is earthy, salty, and tangy. It reminds me of my grandmother's fermented beet borscht. It is a traditional dish in Russia and the Ukraine and the end result of lacto-fermentation. Many folks drink it after a meal, as it aids in digestion. I like to drink it every morning first thing!" —Jeremy Ogusky

....

Yield: 1 quart

¾ lb. (2 large or 3 small) beets, skin on, cut into ½-inch cubes

1 tsp. kosher salt

Water, as needed

Add beets and salt to a clean jar. Fill with water, leaving 1 to 2 inches of headspace. Mix well and stir until the salt is dissolved. Use a canning jar lid and ring to tightly screw on the jar and keep the air out. Store at room temperature, ideally between 60 and 75°F. If you are using a clear glass jar, keep out of direct sunlight or wrap something around the jar, such as a dish towel.

Check on the ferment at least twice a day to burp it and release any carbon dioxide that has built up during fermentation. Stir up the mixture and tighten cap once again. Ferment for 3 days. Strain beets and transfer to a clean, airtight container. Refrigerate once fermentation is complete. Drink within 3 weeks.

NOTES

PICKLED GREEN BEANS

Please note that the type of bean used in this recipe does not have to be specifically a green bean. We grow rattlesnake pole beans in our garden and those are fantastic, so I urge you to use what you have and what is available in your area.

....

Yield: 2 pints

1 lb. green beans (I like to mix green, yellow, and purple beans)
2 cloves garlic, halved
2 tsp. dill seeds
Jalapeños or other spicy peppers (optional)

Brine:

2 cups (5 percent acidity) distilled white vinegar
2 cups water
2 tsp. pickling salt

Wash beans and trim off both ends to fit in the canning jar (about 4 inches for 1 pint jar or 5½ inches for 1 quart-sized jar). In a nonreactive pan, bring the brine ingredients to a boil. Simmer for 3 minutes and turn heat to low.

Divide the garlic and dill seeds between the prepared canning jars. Pack the jars with beans standing on end, without bruising or damaging the beans. If you want spicier beans, add in your hot pepper of choice to the jar (Thai chili peppers or jalapeños work well). Chili pepper flakes will also work if you do not have fresh peppers on hand.

Ladle the hot brine over the beans. Use a funnel to safely transfer the brine into the jar, leaving ½ inch of headspace. Use a nonreactive tool, such as a butter knife, to remove any air bubbles that might be trapped within the beans and the jar. Wipe the rims of the jars with a dampened, clean, lint-free cloth or paper towel and again with a dry towel. Place the canning lid on the jar and twist the canning ring on until it's just-snug on the jar. Process in the water bath for 10 minutes. Carefully remove the jars from the water bath with the canning tongs and place jars on a towel for 12 hours without touching. Allow the beans to pickle at least 2 weeks before tasting so the flavors can meld. Store in the refrigerator after breaking the seal.

NOTES

GREEN BEANS

Sometimes the best recipes are the simplest, and this is one of those instances. These garlicky goodies will have you coming back for more. They have remained a favorite ferment of my daughter's since she was a toddler. Please note that the type of bean used in this recipe does not have to be specifically a green bean. We grow rattlesnake pole beans in our garden and those are fantastic, so I urge you to use what you have and what is available in your area.

....

Yield: 1 quart

½ lb. green beans
1 garlic clove, crushed

Brine:

1 tbsp. kosher salt dissolved in 2 cups water

Wash the beans and trim off the stem-ends to fit in the jar. Place garlic in the bottom of the jar and pack in the beans. Try to get the beans as snug as possible because during fermentation they will shrink a little and begin to float. Once the jar is packed, pour the brine over the beans and submerge them completely.

Use a weight to hold the vegetables underneath the brine. Cover jar/crock with a cheese cloth or other breathable cover to keep dust and bugs from entering your ferment. Store at room temperature, ideally between 60 and 75°F. If you are using a clear jar, keep out of direct sunlight or wrap a dish towel around the jar to keep the light out.

This is a 2-week ferment. Check on the ferment every few days to make sure the brine remains over the beans and that no mold or yeast grows. If the brine is low, press down the weight to bring the brine back over the ferment. Once fermentation is complete, store in an airtight glass jar and refrigerate.

NOTES

GREEN TOMATO SALSA

This recipe is so easy to put together. There is no need to peel the tomatoes, and it tastes excellent freshly made, even before it's cooked and canned!

....

Yield: 4 pints

12 cups fresh green
  tomatoes
2 onions
4 jalapeños
3 garlic cloves
1 cup fresh cilantro
½ cup lime juice
1 tsp. sugar, non-GMO or
  organic
1 tbsp. canning/pickling salt
¼ cup (5 percent acidity)
  distilled white vinegar

Wash and core tomatoes. Rough-chop them until you measure out 12 cups. Use a food processor to chop the tomatoes, onions, jalapeños, garlic, and cilantro. This will likely have to be done in small batches. As each batch is processed, transfer the chopped ingredients to a large, nonreactive pot. Once all vegetables are chopped and in the large pot, add the lime juice, sugar, salt, and vinegar. Mix well and bring to a boil. Simmer for 5 minutes, stirring frequently.

Ladle the hot mixture into prepared jars. Use a funnel to safely transfer the hot salsa mixture into the jars. Leave ½ inch of headspace. Wipe the rims of the jars with a dampened, clean, lint-free cloth or paper towel and again with a dry towel. Place the canning lid on the jar and twist on the canning lid until it's just-snug on the jar. Process in the water bath for 20 minutes. Carefully remove jars from the water bath with the canning tongs and place them on a towel for 12 to 24 hours without touching. Store in the refrigerator after breaking the seal.

NOTES

GREEN TOMATO SALSA

Tearing down the garden at the end of the season won't be as disappointing when you have this salsa to look forward to, made from unripe tomatoes. Use this salsa as you would any traditional red tomato salsa.

....

Yield: 1 quart

6 cups fresh green tomatoes
½ onion, yellow, or purple
2 jalapeños
½ cup cilantro
1 ½ tsp. salt
Fresh lime juice, for serving

If using a food processor, add all the ingredients except the salt and lime. Pulse in food processor a couple of times until the tomatoes are broken down to a salsa consistency. If you do not have access to a food processor, dice the green tomatoes and finely chop the other ingredients by hand. Transfer to a nonreactive bowl, mix in the salt, and stir well.

Transfer salsa to a quart jar and tightly screw on the canning lid and ring to keep the air out. Burp the ferment 1 to 2 times a day; stir up the ferment and press it back down, allowing the carbon dioxide to release, then screw the lid back on.

This salsa is excellent freshly made! As with all ferments, the flavors change during the fermentation process. Taste after 24 hours, again after 48 hours, etc. to determine when it's done to your liking. I ferment this recipe for 3 days.

Mix in freshly squeezed lime juice to salsa before serving. Store in an airtight container after fermentation is complete and refrigerate. Best if eaten within 2 weeks.

NOTES

WATERMELON RIND PICKLES

This recipe comes from the vault of my husband's great-grandma Alice. It is a two-day recipe.

....

Yield: 2 pints

Watermelon rind, peeled
1 cinnamon stick

Overnight soak:

¼ cup pickling salt
3 cups water

Brine:

1 cup (5 percent acidity)
  distilled white vinegar
1 cup water
1 cup sugar, organic or
  non-GMO
1 tsp. ground clove

Wash the skin of the watermelon, dry it off, and cut into quarters. Scrape away the pink juicy fruit, cleaning the pink flesh from the rind as well as possible. A spoon is a great tool to scrape with. Use a potato peeler to peel away the green tough outer layer of the watermelon. Once you have a prepped pale-colored rind, cut the watermelon rind into 1-inch strips and then again into 1-inch squares. Soak in salt water overnight.

The next day, rinse with cold water several times to remove the salt water from the rind. In a medium heavy-bottomed pot, heat the vinegar, water, sugar, and clove and bring to a boil. Boil 5 minutes, stirring frequently. Put the rinsed watermelon rind in a quart jar until it's full to 1 inch below the top of the jar. Fit the cinnamon stick in with the watermelon rind.

Ladle the hot brine over the rind. Use a funnel to safely transfer the brine to the jar. Leave ¼ inch of headspace. Wipe the rim of the jar clean with a dampened lint-free towel or paper towel and again with a dry towel. Place the canning lid on the jar and put the canning ring on until it's just-snug on the jar. Process in the water bath for 10 minutes. Carefully remove the jars from the water bath with the canning tongs and place the jar on a towel for 12 hours without touching. Refrigerate after breaking the seal.

NOTES

WATERMELON RIND PICKLES

Don't let the watermelon rind go to waste! These flavorful pickles are a delicious snack.

....

Yield: 1 pint

Watermelon rind, peeled
1 cinnamon stick

Brine:

2 tsp. kosher salt
1 cup water
½ tsp. ground clove
  (optional)

Wash the skin of the watermelon, dry it off, and cut into quarters. Scrape out the pink juicy fruit and clean the pink flesh off the rind as well as possible. A spoon is a great tool to scrape with. Use a potato peeler to peel away the green, tough, outer layer of the watermelon. Once you have a prepped rind, cut the watermelon rind into 1-inch strips.

Pack a clean pint jar with the watermelon rind and snugly fit in the cinnamon stick. Pour the brine over the watermelon rinds, submerging them completely. Cover the jar with a cheese cloth or other breathable cover to keep dust and bugs from entering the ferment. Store at room temperature, ideally between 60 and 75°F. If you are using a clear glass jar, keep out of direct sunlight or wrap something around the jar, such as a dish towel, to keep the light out. This is a 3-day ferment. Check on the ferment daily to make sure the brine remains over the rind. Once the fermentation is complete, store in an airtight glass jar and refrigerate.

NOTES

PINEAPPLE ZUCCHINI

This recipe was adapted from one on the National Center for Home Food Preservation website when I was looking for a new way to use up excess zucchini. After preservation, the shredded zucchini tastes just like crushed pineapple and can be substituted in recipes that call for regular crushed pineapple.

....

Yield: 3 half pints

4½ cups (2–3 small to medium) zucchini, peeled, shredded

1½ cups unsweetened pineapple juice

½ cup lemon juice

¾ cup sugar

Wash, peel, and shred the zucchini. Use a potato peeler to remove the skin. You may need to peel it twice to get all of the green tint removed from the zucchini. Add zucchini and all other ingredients to a heavy-bottomed saucepan and bring to a boil. Let mixture simmer for 25 minutes, stirring often to avoid burning.

Ladle the hot mixture into prepared jars. Use a funnel to safely transfer the hot pineapple-zucchini mix into jars. Leave ½ inch of headspace. Wipe the rims of the jars with a dampened, clean, lint-free cloth or paper towel and again with a dry towel. Place the canning lid on the jar and twist on the canning ring until it's just-snug on the jar. Process in the water bath for 15 minutes. Carefully remove jars from the water bath with canning tongs and place the jars on a towel for 12 hours without touching. Store in the refrigerator after breaking the seal.

Recipe Variation: Zucchini Pineapple Chunks

Follow the directions referenced above, but instead of shredding the zucchini, remove the seeds and cut them into chunks.

ZUCCHINI-CARROT RELISH

This is an excellent veggie side dish to a meal or great as a topping on a sandwich, burger, or hotdog.

....

Yield: 1 pint

2 medium zucchini, grated

2 carrots, grated, unpeeled

2 garlic cloves, grated or chopped

2 tsp. kosher salt

Grate all veggies. Mix well with kosher salt and pack into a pint jar or other small fermentation vessel. Within 30 minutes or so, there should be enough naturally created brine to cover the vegetables when pushed down with a weight.

Cover the jar with a cheese cloth or other breathable cover to keep dust and bugs from entering the ferment. Store at room temperature, ideally between 60 and 75°F. If you are using a clear glass jar, keep out of direct sunlight or wrap something around the jar, such as a dish towel, to keep the light out.

This is a 3-day ferment. Check on the ferment daily to make sure the brine remains over the grated veggies. If the brine is low, press down on the weight with a clean finger to bring the brine back over the ferment. Once the fermentation is complete, store in an airtight glass jar and refrigerate.

NOTES

FALL & WINTER

CRANBERRY-APPLE JAM

This is an excellent jam to serve in the winter; the taste is truly reminiscent of the holiday season, making it a great holiday gift! I adapted this recipe to use honey instead of additional sugar, and it is even better this way! Any kind of hard or soft apple will work for this recipe. Soft ones break down slightly more than harder apples, while harder ones keep their shape and add a bit more chunkiness to the jam. Same great flavor either way, so you decide!

....

Yield: 4 pints or 8 (8 oz.) jars

8 cups (8 medium or 6 large) apples, peeled, diced

4 cups whole fresh or frozen cranberries

2 cups honey

3 cups sugar, non-GMO or organic

½ cup lemon juice

1 tsp. ground cinnamon

¼ tsp. ground cloves

¼ tsp. ginger (optional)

¼ tsp. nutmeg (optional)

¼ tsp. allspice (optional)

In a large heavy bottomed pot, stir the diced apples, whole cranberries, honey, and sugar together. Bring to a boil. Keep the jam at a medium-high heat for about 12 minutes, stirring frequently until the apples become tender and the cranberries begin to pop.

Add the lemon juice, cinnamon, and cloves. Stir well. Let the mixture simmer until the sauce begins to thicken, about 10 more minutes. I encourage you to take out a spoonful and taste to determine if you want to add more spices.

Ladle the hot jam into warm prepared jars. Use a funnel to safely transfer the sauce, leaving ½ inch of headspace. Wipe the rims of the jars with a dampened, clean, lint-free cloth or paper towel and again with a dry towel. Place the canning lid on the jar and twist the canning ring on until it's just-snug on the jar. Process in the water bath for 10 minutes. Carefully remove the jars from the water bath with canning tongs and place them on a towel for 12 hours without touching. Refrigerate after breaking the seal.

NOTES

CRANBERRIES IN HONEY

Like the Garlic Cloves Fermented in Honey (p. 92), this cranberry-honey ferment is another I've heard a lot about lately. There isn't really a wrong way to make it; you just need to make sure you are checking it daily, whether you use an airlock or a standard canning jar with lid and ring.

·····················

Yield: 1 pint

2 cups whole cranberries
Raw honey, preferably local

Pick through the cranberries and discard any damaged, soft, or unripe berries (pink or green colored). Rinse thoroughly and strain out water. Fill a clean pint jar with cranberries, leave 1 inch of headspace, and stir in honey until the cranberries are submerged. Mix well.

Cover the jar with a canning lid and ring and tightly screw it shut to keep the air out. This ferment needs to be burped daily. Store at room temperature, ideally between 60 and 75°F. If you are using a clear glass jar, keep out of direct sunlight or wrap something around the jar, such as a dish towel, to keep the light out. Ferment 30 days or longer if you prefer. Store in an airtight container once fermentation is complete and refrigerate.

NOTES

CRANBERRY SAUCE

Cranberry sauce is by far one of the easiest canning endeavors you'll partake in. The sauce is full of flavor that cannot compare to any commercially processed sauce. Make a batch of this as a quick side dish over the holidays or gift it to the host of your next family gathering. There will be no disappointing with this vibrant red, sweet, and tart sauce. When serving, consider stirring in nuts, raisins, or some fresh orange zest.

....

Yield: 2–3 pints

8 cups (about 2 pounds) fresh cranberries

2 cups sugar (preferably organic or non-GMO)

2 cups water

¼ tsp. ground allspice (optional)

¼ tsp. ground cloves (optional)

Pick through the cranberries, discarding of any damaged, soft, or unripe berries (pink- or green-colored). Rinse thoroughly and strain out water. In a large heavy-bottomed sauce pan, stir together sugar and water and bring to a boil, stirring until the sugar is dissolved. Add cranberries and bring to a boil. Reduce heat to a medium-high simmer and cook for 10 minutes, stirring occasionally. As the mixture simmers, you will hear the cranberries begin to make popping noises as the skins begin to split apart. At this point, add in ground allspice and ground cloves if desired and stir well.

Ladle the hot berry sauce into warm prepared jars. Use a funnel to safely transfer the sauce, leaving ½ inch of headspace. Wipe the rims of the jars with a dampened, clean, lint-free cloth or paper towel and again with a dry towel. Place the lid on and twist the canning ring on until it's just-snug on the jar. Process in the water bath for 15 minutes. Carefully remove the jars from the water bath with canning tongs and place them on a towel for 12 hours without touching. Refrigerate after breaking the seal.

NOTES

Day 1   Day 3

CRANBERRY-ORANGE RELISH

This cranberry ferment is full of flavor. The deep red color will liven up any plate. This sweet and citrusy relish is a fermented version of my mother-in-law's favorite Thanksgiving side dish.

....

Yield: 1 pint

3 cups whole cranberries
½ tsp. organic orange zest
2 tbsp. fresh squeezed
    orange juice
2 tbsp. raw honey

Pick through the cranberries and discard any damaged, soft, or unripe berries (pink- or green-colored). Rinse thoroughly and strain out water. Use a food processor to chop the cranberries; it only takes 2 to 3 seconds. Transfer berries into a pint jar and add in orange zest, juice, and honey. Mix together well.

Use a canning jar lid and ring to tightly shut the jar and keep the air out. Check on the ferment once a day by removing the lid and stirring the cranberry mixture, patting it back down, placing the lid back on, and tightly closing. This is a 3-day ferment. Refrigerate after fermentation is complete. Best if used within 2 weeks.

NOTES

PUMPKIN BUTTER

This recipe is inspired by my mother's delicious homemade pumpkin pies that she makes every fall with her homegrown pie pumpkins. Reserve the seeds to make baked pumpkin seeds—such a tasty treat!

....

Yield: 1 pint

1 small (3–4 lb.) sugar pumpkin, peeled, chopped to make 4½ cups

1 cup water

⅛ tsp. salt

1 tsp. ground cinnamon

¼ cup maple syrup

2 tbsp. organic apple cider vinegar

1 tbsp. lemon juice

½ tsp. ground ginger

½ tsp. ground nutmeg (optional)

½ tsp. ground allspice (optional)

Prepare the pumpkin by washing, cutting off both ends, cutting in half, and scooping out seeds and membranes. Use a spoon to scrape the inside clean. Use a potato peeler to peel off the thick, tough pumpkin skin. Once cleaned and peeled, cut the pumpkin into 1-inch thick strips and again into 1-inch cubes.

Put all ingredients into a large heavy-bottomed pot, mix well, and bring to a simmer. Cover and simmer 20 to 30 minutes, stirring often to avoid burning. Once pumpkin is tender and easily broken with a wooden spoon or other utensil, remove the pot from heat and let cool for a couple of minutes. Using an immersion hand blender or other blender, purée the pumpkin mixture for several minutes into a smooth and silky consistency; be careful not to splash any mixture on yourself.

Once puréed, carefully ladle the hot pumpkin butter into a prepared canning or other airtight jar; use a spatula to scrape the pot clean. This is not a water bath recipe, as creating shelf-stable pumpkin recipe would require a pressure cooker. Once cooled, refrigerate up to two weeks.

NOTES

SUGAR PUMPKIN KVASS

Pumpkin kvass isn't a common kvass, so when I experimented with it, I was pleasantly surprised by the lightly flavorful, bubbly drink.

....

Yield: 1 quart

1–2 cups pumpkin scraps (seeds, skin, pumpkin, and pulp)
1 tbsp. raw honey
1 tsp. kosher salt
1 tbsp. fresh ginger, grated or finely chopped (optional)
Water, as needed

Fill a quart jar ⅓ full of pumpkin scraps. Fill with water to 1 inch from the top. Stir in honey, salt, and ginger. Mix well.

Use a canning jar lid and ring to tightly screw on the jar to keep the air out. Store at room temperature, ideally between 60 and 75°F. If you are using a clear glass jar, keep out of direct sunlight or wrap something around the jar, such as a dish towel. Check on the ferment at least twice a day to burp it and release any carbon dioxide that has built up during fermentation. Stir up the mixture and tighten cap once again. Ferment 4 to 5 days. Strain out pumpkin pieces before drinking. Refrigerate once fermentation is complete. Drink within 2 weeks.

NOTES

SUGAR PUMPKIN PICKLES

....

Yield: 1 pint

½ small (3–4 lb.) sugar
pumpkin, cubed to make
1½ cups
Cinnamon stick (optional)
½ tsp. ground nutmeg
(optional)

Brine:

1 tsp. kosher salt, dissolved
in 1 cup water

Prepare the pumpkin by washing, cutting off both ends, cutting in half, and scooping out seeds and membranes. Use a spoon to scrape the inside clean. Use a potato peeler to peel off the thick, tough pumpkin skin. Once cleaned and peeled, cut the pumpkin into 1½-inch thick strips and again into 1½-inch cubes.

Pack the jar with the pumpkin and optional ingredients, if you choose. Pour the prepared brine over the pumpkin cubes until it covers them completely. If the squash does not stay under the brine, add a weight to hold it down. Cover the jar with a cheese cloth or other breathable cover to keep dust and bugs from entering the ferment. Store at room temperature, ideally between 60 and 75°F. If you are using a clear glass jar, keep out of direct sunlight or wrap something around the jar, such as a dish towel, to keep the light out.

This is a 3-day ferment. Check on the ferment daily to make sure the brine remains over the squash. If the brine is low, press down on the weight with a clean finger to bring the brine back over the ferment. Once the fermentation is complete, store in a glass airtight jar and refrigerate.

NOTES

QUICK APPLESAUCE

No food mill required for this quick applesauce recipe!

....

Yield: 1 pint, plus a little extra to store in the fridge

3 lb. (6-8 cups) apples, peeled, diced
¼ cup honey
¼ cup water
¼ cup lemon juice
1 tsp. ground cinnamon (optional)

Add all ingredients to a large heavy-bottomed pot, mix ingredients together, bring heat to medium-high, and simmer covered for 20 minutes. Stir often to avoid burning.

Once apples are soft, turn off heat and let the apples cool off for a couple of minutes. Use an immersion hand blender or other blender to break down the apples into the consistency you prefer for apple sauce.

Ladle the hot apple mixture in jars. Use a funnel to safely transfer the sauce into each jar, leaving ½ inch of headspace. Use a spatula to scrape the pot clean. Wipe the rims of the jars clean with a dampened clean paper towel or lint-free cloth and then again with a dry towel and place the lid on. Put jar ring on until it's just-snug on the jar. Process in the water bath for 10 minutes. Carefully remove the jar from the water bath with canning tongs and place them on a towel for 12 hours without touching. Refrigerate after breaking the seal.

NOTES

APPLESAUCE

This is an extremely simple recipe that yields a delicious fermented applesauce.

....

Yield: 1 pint

3 organic apples, cored and
   rough-chopped
⅛ tsp. kosher salt
½ tsp. ground cinnamon
   (optional)

Put apples into a food processor and purée until apples are broken down into a smooth applesauce consistency. I like to leave the skins on, but removing the skins before puréeing will result in a smoother applesauce. Transfer applesauce into a clean pint jar and stir in salt and optional cinnamon, if desired. Mix well. Use a canning jar lid and ring to tightly screw on the jar to keep the air out. Store at room temperature, ideally between 60 and 75°F.

Check on the ferment once a day by removing the lid and stirring the applesauce, placing the lid back on, and tightly closing. Keep ferment out of direct sunlight or wrap a dish towel around the jar to keep light out. This is a 3-day ferment. Refrigerate for up to 2 weeks.

NOTES

CINNAMON-HONEY APPLE BUTTER

Apple butter is ridiculously versatile. It's great on pancakes, cheese, oatmeal, buttered toast, and even pork chops! It's a recipe that I was turned off by for many years because every recipe I found required a crockpot, food mill, additional pectin, or an entire day of cooking. I knew there had to be a quicker way, so I developed this delicious and easy apple butter recipe.

....

Yield: 4 half-pint jam jars or 2 pints

3 lb. (8-9 cups chopped) apples, cored, cubed

¼ tsp. salt

2 tbsp. lemon juice

¼ cup organic apple cider vinegar

1 cup water

1 ½ tsp. ground cinnamon

¼ tsp. ground cloves

¼ cup raw honey

¼ cup brown sugar, loosely packed

¼ tsp. vanilla extract (optional)

⅛ tsp. ground allspice (optional)

Add apples, salt, lemon juice, apple cider vinegar, water, and cinnamon to a large heavy-bottomed pot. Mix ingredients together, cover, and bring to medium heat. Simmer covered for 20 minutes, stirring occasionally.

Once apples are soft and can be easily smashed with a spoon or fork, remove from heat and let the apples cool off for a couple of minutes. Using an immersion hand blender or other blender, purée the apples for 1 to 2 minutes into a smooth and silky consistency; be careful not to splash any hot apple mixture on yourself. Add in ground cloves, honey, brown sugar, and optional ingredients, if desired. Use a clean spoon to scoop out a small sample to taste what ingredients you'd like to add more of. Mix well and return pot to a simmer, uncovered. Simmer on low for 20 minutes to 1 hour, stirring frequently to avoid burning the apple mixture. The length of time to simmer depends on the type of apple used. Some apples create a nice thick sauce after just 20 minutes, while others take 30 to 60 minutes. Generally, by 30 minutes, most sauces will be thick enough to can. I determine thickness by eyeballing the sauce; I can just tell, but for those that don't quite have an eye for it yet, thickness can be tested like this: take a small spoonful of the apple mixture and put it in a glass or ceramic bowl. Put the bowl in the fridge for 5 to 10 minutes to cool. Once cooled, turn the bowl on its side and the sauce should not move, or move very little. If your sauce does this, it has reached the correct thickness and is ready to can.

Ladle the hot apple mixture into jars, using a funnel to safely transfer the sauce into each jar. Leave ½-inch headspace. Use a spatula to scrape the pot clean; it's surprising how much apple butter sticks to the pan because of how thick it is. Wipe the rims of the jars clean with a dampened clean paper towel or lint-free cloth and then again with a dry towel and place the lid on. Put jar ring on until it's just-snug on the jar. Process in the water bath for 10 minutes. Carefully remove jars from the water bath with canning tongs and place them on a towel for 12 hours without touching. Refrigerate after breaking the seal.

SPICY PICKLED CALIFORNIA MIX

....

Yield: 2 pints

2 cups cauliflower florets

6 serrano peppers, sliced
 into ¼-inch pieces

4 garlic cloves, chopped

2 celery stalks, sliced into
 ¼-inch pieces

2 carrots, sliced or julienned

½ cup red bell pepper,
 chopped

Brine:

2 cups (5 percent acidity)
 distilled white vinegar

1 cup water

1 tbsp. canning salt

1 tsp. dried oregano
 (optional)

Clean and prepare all vegetables. In a large nonreactive pot, bring the brine ingredients to a boil. Once salt is dissolved, add the chopped veggies and bring the mixture back to a boil. Boil on medium-high for 3 minutes and reduce heat to low.

Ladle the hot vegetable mixture into the prepared jars. Use a funnel to safely transfer the mixture into the jars, leaving ¼-inch headspace. Wipe the rims of the jars with a dampened, clean, lint-free cloth or paper towel and then again with a dry towel. Put the canning lid on the jar and then twist on the canning ring until it is just-snug on the jar. Process in the water bath for 10 minutes. Carefully remove the jars from the water bath with the canning tongs and place the jars on a towel for 12 hours without touching. Let the vegetable mixture sit for 2 weeks before opening so the flavors have a chance to meld. Refrigerate after breaking the seal.

NOTES

GIARDINIERA

This is by far one of my favorite ferments. I love adding this spicy veggie mix to sandwiches, chili, eggs, pizza, pasta—pretty much everything.

....

Yield: 1 quart

¼ cup (1 whole) carrot, unpeeled, chopped

½ cup (2 stalks) celery, sliced into ¼-inch pieces

2 cloves garlic, chopped

½ cup (6 whole) serrano peppers, sliced into ¼-inch pieces

½ cup cauliflower florets

1 grape leaf (optional)

Brine:

1 tbsp. kosher salt, dissolved in 2 cups water

Chop up all vegetables, mix together, and transfer to a quart jar or other fermentation vessel. A grape leaf will help keep the vegetables crunchy, but it is not required. Pour brine over the vegetables, completely covering the mixture by ½ to 1 inch, and use a weight to hold the veggies under the brine. Leave space for the veggies to bubble. This is a very active ferment, so expect a lot of bubbles.

Cover jar with a cheese cloth or other breathable cover to keep dust and bugs from entering your ferment. Store at room temperature, ideally between 60 and 75°F. If you are using a clear jar, keep out of direct sunlight or wrap a dish towel around the jar to block out light. This is a 7-day ferment. Be sure to check on the ferment every day to make sure the brine remains over the mix and that no mold or yeast has begun to grow. If the brine is low, press down the weight to bring the brine back over the ferment. Once fermentation is complete, store in an airtight glass container and refrigerate.

NOTES

DILLED ONION RINGS

My husband's grandma Elsie turned ninety this year. She is such an elegant woman and very fun to talk to. She has the best memory of anyone I know and can remember specific details such as the avenues that her friends lived on in the fifties. I'm always very impressed with her knack for detail—it's one of the things I admire most about her. She grew up in a time where canning was not a hobby, but a requirement, and was kind enough to share a few of her mother's hand-written recipes with me for this book. These dilled onion rings are one of her most cherished recipes.

....

Yield: 1 pint

2 cups (2 whole) yellow onions, thinly sliced
2 sprigs fresh dill weed

Brine:

½ cup sugar, non-GMO or organic
1 cup (5 percent acidity) distilled white vinegar
1 tbsp. pickling salt
¼ tsp. whole peppercorns (optional)

Pack jar with onions and dill. In a nonreactive pot, bring the brine ingredients to a boil for 3 minutes, stirring until the salt and sugar is dissolved, then reduce heat to a low simmer.

Ladle the hot brine over the onions. Use a funnel to safely transfer the brine into the jar, leaving ½ inch of headspace. Use a nonreactive tool, such as a butter knife, to remove any air bubbles that may be trapped within the onions and the jar. Wipe the rims of the jars with a dampened, clean, lint-free cloth or paper towel and then again with a dry towel. Place the canning lid on and twist the canning ring on until it's just-snug on the jar. Process in the water bath for 10 minutes. Carefully remove the jar from the water bath with the canning tongs and place on a towel for 12 hours without touching. Refrigerate after breaking the seal.

NOTES

RED ONIONS

These onions are excellent in sandwiches (especially pulled pork or burgers), served over fish, added to salads, or used as a garnish for tacos!

....

Yield: 1 quart

1 large red onion, sliced
1 bay leaf
½ tsp. whole black peppercorns
2 cloves garlic, crushed

Brine:

1 tbsp. of salt dissolved in 2 cups water

Peel onion and slice into ¼-inch slices. Pack jar with ingredients, adding the peppercorns and garlic at the bottom and tucking the bay leaf on the side without breaking it. Pour the brine over the onions until they are completely submerged. Leave 1½ inches of headspace for the weight, brine, and room for the ferment to bubble.

Use a weight to hold the onions underneath the brine. Cover jar/crock with a cheese cloth or other breathable cover to keep dust and bugs from entering your ferment. Store at room temperature, ideally between 60 and 75°F. If you are using a clear jar, keep out of direct sunlight or wrap a dish towel around the vessel.

This is a 7-day ferment. Be sure to check on the ferment every couple of days to make sure the brine remains over the onions. If the brine is low, press down the weight to bring the brine back over the ferment. Once fermentation is complete, store in an airtight glass jar and refrigerate.

PICKLED WATERMELON RADISHES

The brine of this radish pickle turns into the most beautiful shade of red after the water bath. These are great on sandwiches, chopped up in salads, or eaten as is.

....

Yield: 1 pint

2–3 watermelon radishes, sliced into ¼-inch pieces
1 tsp. whole black peppercorns
1 garlic clove, sliced (optional)
1 jalapeño, sliced (optional)

Brine:

½ cup (5 percent acidity) distilled white vinegar
½ cup water
1 tsp. canning salt

Wash the radishes and trim off the ends. Depending on the size of the radish, you can either leave the slices whole or cut them in half. Add in peppercorns and optional ingredients, if desired, and pack the radish slices snugly into a prepared canning jar. In a nonreactive pot, bring the brine ingredients to a boil and simmer for 3 minutes, then reduce heat to a low simmer.

Ladle the hot brine over the radishes. Use a funnel to safely transfer the brine into the jar, leaving ½ inch of headspace. Use a nonreactive tool, such as a butter knife, to remove any air bubbles that might be trapped within the jar. Wipe the rims of the jar with a dampened, clean, lint-free cloth or paper towel and again with a dry towel. Place the canning lid on the jar and twist on the canning ring until it's just-snug on the jar. Process in the water bath for 10 minutes. Carefully remove the jar from the water bath with the canning tongs and place on a towel for 12 hours without touching. Refrigerate once the seal is broken.

NOTES

WATERMELON RADISH PICKLES

You'd never know the beauty hidden within this radish by looking at it from the outside. I prefer these radishes to regular red table radishes because their flavor is milder and they are much prettier. The inside is bright pink, which causes the brine to turn a lovely shade of pink.

....

Yield: 1 pint

1–2 watermelon radishes, thinly sliced

Brine:

1 tsp. salt dissolved in 2 cups water

Wash the radish, trim off the ends. Depending on the size of the radish, you can either leave the slices whole or cut them in half. Stack them in the jar, leaving 1½ inches of room for a weight, brine, and space for the ferment to bubble. Once the jar is packed, pour the brine over the radish slices, covering them completely.

Use a weight to hold the radish slices underneath the brine. Cover jar with cheese cloth or other breathable cover to keep dust and bugs from entering your ferment. Store at room temperature, ideally between 60 and 75°F. If you are using a clear jar, keep out of direct sunlight or wrap a dish towel around it.

This is a 4-day ferment. Be sure to check on the ferment every day to make sure the brine remains over the radish slices and no mold or yeast forms. If the brine is low, press down the weight to bring the brine back over the ferment. Once fermentation is complete, store in an airtight glass jar and refrigerate.

NOTES

SUNCHOKES

To make recipe with fresh turmeric, just wash as much as you'd like to add, slice it into similar thickness as the sunchokes, and pack it into the jar with the raw sunchokes.

....

Yield: 2 pints

4 cups sunchokes,
   sliced into ¼-inch coins
2 garlic cloves, halved
¼ tsp. coriander seeds
1 tsp. yellow mustard seeds
1 tsp. crushed red pepper
   flakes

Brine:

1½ cup (5 percent acidity)
   distilled white vinegar
1 cup water
1½ tsp. canning salt
1 tbsp. sugar, non-GMO or
   organic
2 tsp. turmeric powder or
   fresh turmeric

Wash the sunchokes under cold water and use a vegetable scrubber to clean the skin. If the sunchoke is thick, cut it in half lengthwise and slice. In a nonreactive saucepan, bring the brine ingredients to a boil and simmer for 3 minutes. Divide the garlic, coriander seeds, mustard seeds, and red pepper flakes between the jars. Fill the jars with sunchokes, trying to fit them in as snug as possible without crushing them.

Ladle the hot brine over the sunchokes. Use a funnel to safely transfer the brine into each jar, leaving ½ inch of headspace. Use a stainless-steel butter knife or other nonreactive tool to remove any air bubbles trapped inside the jar. Wipe the rims of the jars with a dampened, clean, lint-free cloth or paper towel and again with a dry towel and place the canning lid on. Twist the canning ring on until it's just-snug on the jar. Process in the water bath canner for 10 minutes. Carefully remove the jars from the water bath with canning tongs and place the jars on a towel for 12 hours without touching. Store in the refrigerator after breaking the seal.

NOTES

SUNCHOKES WITH TURMERIC

Fermented sunchokes keep their delicious crunch, similar to the crispness of water chestnuts.

....

Yield: I quart

I garlic clove, crushed
2 cups sunchokes, unpeeled,
   sliced into coins

Brine:

I tbsp. salt dissolved into
   2 cups water
I tsp. turmeric powder

Add garlic and sliced sunchokes into a clean jar or crock. Pour the brine over the sunchokes, leaving 1½ inches of headspace.

Use a weight to hold the vegetables underneath the brine. Cover jar/crock with a cheese cloth or other breathable cover to keep dust and bugs from entering your ferment. Store at room temperature, ideally between 60 and 75°F. If you are using a clear jar, keep out of direct sunlight or wrap a dish towel around it. This is an 8-day ferment. Be sure to check on the ferment every couple of days to make sure the brine remains over the sunchokes and that no mold or yeast forms. If the brine is low, press down the weight to bring the brine back over the ferment. Once fermentation is complete, store in an airtight glass jar and refrigerate.

NOTES

SAUERKRAUT: STEP-BY-STEP

1.

Remove outer layers of the cabbage, wash, halve, remove core, and shred into thin, uniform slices so the kraut ferments evenly.

2.

Mix in salt.

3.

4.

Use your fist or other tool to tightly pack the cabbage down into your fermentation vessel of choice.

5.

SAUERKRAUT

When most people think about fermented foods, their mind immediately jumps to beer or sauerkraut. Sauerkraut is one of the most iconic fermented foods out there. It's a staple of many people's diets around the world. If everyone knew how easy it was to make themselves, they would never buy it from the store again. For years, I made sauerkraut by cutting the cabbages up, massaging in the salt, and packing my crock full—all by hand. This is a classic and simple technique, and it's a great way to do it when you are beginning. But if you know you are going to make kraut consistently throughout the year and have committed to making the awesomeness it entails on a regular basis, then I highly recommend purchasing a cabbage shredder or hunting one down at a garage sale. It turns a thirty-minute task into a 3- or 4-minute task. Not only does it speed up the process enormously, it shreds the cabbage into the perfect-sized shred for sauerkraut (or coleslaw, for that matter). If your batch of sauerkraut has a lot of liquid leftover, don't toss it—drink it! That leftover juice is what is popularly known as a "gut shot." It's filled with lots of probiotics and vitamin C, is said to be a hangover cure, and, heck, it tastes surprisingly good. If you aren't a fan of drinking the brine, marinate meat with it or use it to make a delicious salad dressing.

....

Yield: 3 pints

2–3 heads organic cabbage

2 tbsp. kosher salt

Remove the outer leaves from the cabbage and discard. Wash the cabbage with cold water. Cut each cabbage in half and remove the core from each half. Shred the cabbages into thinly sliced pieces, about ⅛-to-¼-inches thick. Once both cabbages are shredded, put the shreds in a large glass bowl or other nonreactive bowl. Mix the salt in with the cabbage shreds and massage the salt into the shreds. Transfer the mixture into a crock or jar, pushing down the cabbage mixture as you pack the vessel. I have a wooden kraut pounder (also known as a cabbage tamper/masher/pounder) for this task that helps me get leverage with the tool and really pack the crock/jars tightly full of cabbage and release any liquid from the cabbage.

I typically use a gallon-sized crock for this size of a batch, which would translate to 2 quart jars or 1 gallon jar. Within 1 hour, all the cabbage should be packed into your fermenting vessel(s), and enough brine should be naturally created to cover the cabbage shreds.

If there is not enough brine to cover the cabbage, mix extra brine (dissolve 1 tbsp. with 2 cups water) and add it to the jar/crock until the cabbage shreds are covered.

Use a weight to hold the vegetables underneath the brine. Cover jar/crock with a cheese cloth or another breathable cover to keep dust and bugs from entering your ferment. Store at room temperature, ideally between 60 and 75°F.

This is a 3-to-5-week ferment. Be sure to check on the ferment every few days to make sure the brine remains over the cabbage and that no mold has begun to form. It is completely normal to see little bubbles or even foam-like bubbling occur at the top of the ferment. If the brine is low, press down the weight to bring the brine back over the ferment. If there is not enough brine, add more as referenced above. Weekly taste testing is recommended to determine which flavor you prefer as the ferment changes throughout the process. Once fermentation is complete, store in airtight glass jars and refrigerate.

Recipe Variation: Purple Kraut

Mix one head of green cabbage with one head of red or purple cabbage and follow the Sauerkraut directions fully. The combination of the two cabbages makes a stunning pink sauerkraut that livens up every plate!

Recipe Variation: Beet Kraut

Follow the Sauerkraut recipe above, but add one grated beet into the cabbage and salt mixture. Wash the beet and trim off the ends before grating, but leave the skin on. The addition of the beet will make a beautiful deep pink/purple sauerkraut that has a hint of beet flavor. It's gorgeous *and* delicious!

SAUERKRAUT WITH CARAWAY SEEDS

This recipe can be made without caraway seeds as well: just follow processing directions without adding the seeds. If you prefer more of a caraway seed presence, try lightly toasting the seeds in a frying pan before mixing them in with the sauerkraut. Fermented, unprocessed kraut is more beneficial to your health because it's full of healthy-belly bacteria that, once water bath is processed, are killed off. However, it is nice to have on hand when needed so it's worth making a few jars shelf-stable. To make canned sauerkraut, you must first ferment the cabbage.

....

Yield: 3 pints

2 heads organic cabbage

2 tbsp. kosher salt

1 tsp. caraway seeds, per pint

Remove the outer leaves from the cabbage and discard. Wash the cabbage with cold water. Cut each cabbage in half and remove the core from each half. Shred the cabbages into thinly sliced pieces, about ⅛-to-¼-inches thick. Once both cabbages are shredded, put the shreds in a large glass bowl or other nonreactive bowl. Mix the salt in with the cabbage shreds and massage the salt into the shreds. Transfer the mixture into a crock or jar, pushing down the cabbage mixture as you pack the vessel. I have a wooden kraut pounder (also known as a cabbage tamper/masher/pounder) for this task that helps me get leverage with the tool and really pack the crock/jars tightly full of cabbage and release any liquid from the cabbage.

I typically use a gallon-sized crock for this size of a batch, which would translate to 2 quart jars or 1 gallon jar. Within 1 hour, all the cabbage should be packed into your fermenting vessel(s), and enough brine should be naturally created to cover the cabbage shreds.

If there is not enough brine to cover the cabbage, mix extra brine (dissolve 1 tbsp. with 2 cups water) and add it to the jar/crock until the cabbage shreds are covered.

Use a weight to hold the vegetables underneath the brine. Cover jar/crock with a cheese cloth or another breathable cover to keep dust and bugs from entering your ferment. Store at room temperature, ideally between 60 and 75°F.

This is a 3-to-5-week ferment. Be sure to check on the ferment every few days to make sure the brine remains over the cabbage and that no mold has begun to form. It is completely normal to see little bubbles or even foam-like bubbling occur at the top of the ferment. If the brine is low, press down the weight to bring the brine back over the ferment. If there is not enough brine, add more as referenced above. Weekly taste testing is recommended to determine which flavor you prefer as the ferment changes throughout the process.

After cabbage ferments to your liking, use a measuring cup to determine how much sauerkraut you have and ultimately how many pint or quart jars you will need to prepare for this recipe. Heat sauerkraut and caraway seeds in a heavy-bottomed, nonreactive pot and bring to a boil. Stir often to avoid burning the kraut. Once heated thoroughly, simmer for 5 minutes and reduce heat to low. Disperse sauerkraut into the prepared canning jars. Use a funnel to safely transfer the kraut into the jars, leaving ½-inch headspace. Use a stainless-steel butter knife or other similar tool to rid of any air bubbles trapped within the sauerkraut and the jar. Wipe the rims of the jars with a dampened, clean, lint-free cloth or paper towel and again with a dry towel. Place the canning lid on the jar and twist the canning ring on until it's just-snug on the jar. Process pints in the water bath for 10 minutes and quarts for 15 mins. Carefully remove the jars from the water bath with the canning tongs and place jars on a towel for 12-hours without touching. Refrigerate after breaking the seal.

NOTES

QUICK CURTIDO

Curtido is a traditional El Salvadorian cabbage salad. It can be eaten any way that you'd normally enjoy sauerkraut, but it's also phenomenal added to tacos. I keep finding new ways to incorporate this delicious ferment to my everyday meals.

....

Yield: 1 quart

1 head organic green cabbage

3 carrots, grated

1 onion, thinly sliced

2 jalapeños, thinly sliced

1 tsp. fresh lime juice

1½ tbsp. kosher salt

In a large glass bowl, mix together all grated and sliced veggies together with lime juice and massage with salt. I have a small 2.5-liter crock that I use when making small batches. If you do not have a small crock, use a glass quart canning jar.

Within an hour, all the shredded vegetables should be packed into your fermenting vessel(s), and enough brine should be created to cover the cabbage shreds. If there is not enough brine to cover the cabbage, mix extra brine (dissolve 1 tbsp. with 2 cups water) and add it to the jar/crock until the cabbage shreds are covered. Use a weight to hold the vegetables underneath the brine. Cover jar/crock with a cheese cloth or another breathable cover to keep dust and bugs from entering your ferment. Store at room temperature, ideally between 60 and 75°F.

This is a 10-to-12-day ferment. Be sure to check on the ferment every few days to make sure the brine remains over the cabbage and that no mold has begun to form. It is completely normal to see little bubbles or even foam-like bubbling occur at the top of the ferment. If the brine is low, press down the weight to bring the brine back over the ferment. If there is not enough brine, add more as referenced above. Taste test after 7 days to determine if the flavor is ideal or if you'd like to ferment a few more days. Once fermentation is complete, store in glass, airtight jars and refrigerate.

NOTES

SPICY CURRIED-CAULIFLOWER PICKLES

Super delicious, zingy cauliflower pickles with a mild spice.

....

Yield: 2 pints

4 cups cauliflower florets

2 bay leaves

½ tsp. celery seeds

2 tsp. crushed red pepper flakes or more for extra spice

Brine:

2 cups (5 percent acidity) distilled white vinegar

1 cup water

2 tsp. curry powder

1 tsp. canning salt

Clean cauliflower and cut away bite-size pieces of the florets. It will take about ½ a cauliflower to fill 2 pints. In a nonreactive pot, prepare the brine. Bring to a boil and simmer 3 minutes until the salt is dissolved, then turn the brine down to low.

Divide the bay leaves, celery seeds, and crushed red pepper flakes between the jars. Pack the jars with cauliflower and carefully ladle the hot brine over, leaving ½ inch of headspace. Use a funnel to safely transfer the brine to each jar. Wipe the rims of the jars with a dampened, clean, lint-free cloth or paper towel and once again with a dry towel. Place the canning lid on the jar and twist on the canning ring until it's just snug on the jar. Process in the water bath canner for 10 minutes. Carefully remove the jars from the water bath with the canning tongs and place on a towel for 12 hours without touching. Allow the cauliflower to pickle for at least 1 week before opening. Store in the refrigerator after the seal is broken.

NOTES

CAULIFLOWER WITH TURMERIC

This cauliflower ferment is another one of my favorite ferments. The cauliflower keeps a nice crunch after fermentation and has excellent flavor. This recipe can also be made with fresh turmeric.

....

Yield: 1 quart

3½ cups cauliflower florets
4 garlic cloves, slivered
2 jalapeños, stems removed,
  sliced

Brine:

1 tsp. kosher salt
2 tsp. ground or fresh
  turmeric
2 cups water

Wash cauliflower and cut the florets in uniform-sized pieces so they ferment evenly. In a large bowl, mix the cauliflower, garlic, and jalapeños together. Transfer the cauliflower mixture to a clean quart jar or other fermentation vessel.

Once the jar/vessel is packed, pour the brine over, making sure to submerge the veggies completely. Leave space for a weight and space for the ferment to bubble. Cover the jar/vessel with a cheese cloth or other breathable cover to keep dust and bugs from entering the ferment. Store at room temperature, ideally between 60 and 75°F. If you are using a clear jar, wrap a towel around the jar to keep light out. This is a 6-day ferment. Check on the ferment every day to make sure the brine remains over the veggies and that no mold or yeast forms. If the brine is low, press down on the weight to bring the brine back over the ferment. Once fermentation is complete, store in an airtight glass container and refrigerate.

NOTES

BUTTERNUT SQUASH

These tasty squash bites are great as a stand-alone snack and taste delicious blended up in a smoothie, diced up in a fruit salad, or served with fish.

....

Yield: 1 quart

3½ cups butternut squash, skin removed, cubed

2 whole cinnamon sticks

Brine:

1 tbsp. kosher salt dissolved in 2 cups water

Fill a quart-sized jar with the cubed squash. Fit 2 cinnamon sticks in with the cubes, and try to wedge them in so they do not float to the top. Pour the brine over the squash until it covers them. If the squash will not stay under the brine on their own, add a weight to hold them down. Cover the jar with a cheese cloth or other breathable cover to keep dust and bugs from entering the ferment. Store at room temperature, ideally between 60 and 75°F. If you are using a clear glass jar, keep out of direct sunlight or wrap something around the jar, such as a dish towel, to keep the light out. This is a 3-day ferment. Check on the ferment daily to make sure the brine remains over the squash. If the brine is low, press down on the weight with a clean finger to bring the brine back over the ferment. Once the fermentation is complete, store in a glass, airtight jar and refrigerate.

NOTES

PICKLED BRUSSELS SPROUTS

Pickled Brussels sprouts are one of the items on my annual "must-make" list. If we don't have a fresh vegetable side to eat with dinner, I pull these out. My husband and daughter don't typically like Brussels sprouts, but they love them pickled. They are also incredibly delicious garnishes for Bloody Marys and make unique gifts. Regular-mouth jars are recommended for this recipe, as they help keep the Brussels sprouts pushed down in the jar.

....

Yield: 2 pints

3 cups Brussels sprouts
6 garlic cloves, sliced
2 tsp. yellow mustard seeds
2 tsp. red pepper flakes
   (optional)

Brine:

2 cups water
2 cups (5 percent acidity)
   white distilled vinegar
2 tbsp. pickling salt

Baby Brussels sprouts are preferable for this recipe, but medium ones will do. Clean the Brussels sprouts by soaking them, trimming off the ends, and removing the outer layers of leaves. Cut off any blemishes. Cut larger Brussels sprouts in half. In a nonreactive pot, bring the brine ingredients to a boil for 3 minutes, then reduce heat to a low simmer.

Divide the garlic between the jars. Pack the jars with Brussels sprouts and try to fit them in snugly. Divide the mustard seeds and optional hot pepper flakes, if desired, between the jars. Ladle the hot brine over the Brussels sprouts. Use a funnel to safely transfer the brine into each jar, leaving ½ inch of headspace. Use a nonreactive tool, such as a butter knife, to remove any air bubbles that may be trapped within the jar and sprouts. Wipe the rims of the jars with a dampened, clean, lint-free cloth or paper towel and again with a dry towel. Place the canning lid on the jar and twist canning ring on until it's just-snug on the jar. Process in the water bath for 10 minutes. Carefully remove the jars from the water bath with the canning tongs and place on a towel for 12 hours without touching. Allow the Brussels sprouts to pickle at least 2 weeks before tasting so the flavors have a chance to meld. Store in the refrigerator after breaking the seal.

BRUSSELS SPROUTS

These little mini cabbages take quite a while to ferment, but they are worth the wait! If impatient, you can shred the Brussels sprouts, but be sure to begin taste testing them after two weeks to determine if the flavor you are looking for has been reached. If not, ferment a few more days and taste again.

....

Yield: I quart

I lb. Brussels sprouts, halved
I tsp. whole peppercorns
2 garlic cloves, crushed

Brine:

I tbsp. salt, dissolved
    in 2 cups water

Baby Brussels sprouts are preferable for this recipe, but medium ones will do. Clean the Brussels sprouts by soaking them, trimming off the ends, and removing the outer layers of leaves. Cut off any blemishes. Cut larger Brussels sprouts in half. Pack the peppercorns, sprouts, and garlic in a clean quart jar, leaving 1½ inches of headspace. Pour the brine over the sprouts, submerging them completely.

Cover the jar/vessel with a cheese cloth or other breathable cover to keep dust and bugs from entering the ferment. Store at room temperature, ideally between 60 and 75°F. If you are using a clear jar, wrap a dish towel around the jar to keep light out. This is a 4-week ferment. Check on the ferment every day to make sure the brine remains over the veggies and that no mold or yeast forms. If the brine is low, press down on the weight to bring the brine back over the ferment. Once fermentation is complete, store in an airtight glass container and refrigerate.

NOTES

NOTES

NOTES

NOTES

NOTES

RESOURCES

....

Canning

National Center for Home Preservation: Nchfp.uga.edu

Fermentation

Stone Creek Trading: Stonecreektrading.com

Various-sized crocks in a variety of styles, crock weights, cabbage shredders, cabbage corers, cabbage pounders, and other supplies.

Ogusky Ceramics: Clayrocks.com

Beautifully hand-crafted pottery fermentation crocks.

Pickl-It: Pickl-it.com

A great resource for glass jars with airlocks.

Wild Fermentation: The Flavor, Nutrition, and Craft of Live-Culture Foods by Sandor Katz
This book goes into depth about the process of fermentation, as well as the history, and offers recipes for vegetables but also cheese, yogurt, bread, and more.

Both

Amazon: Amazon.com
Most everything on the supply lists for canning and fermenting can be found at Amazon.com.

MightyNest: Mightynest.com
Lovely online shop that sells only safe products, free of harsh chemicals. Wonderful place to buy glass jars for canning and fermenting, as well as other kitchen basics and common household goods.

Minnesota from Scratch: MinnesotafromScratch.wordpress.com
Facebook: Minnesota from Scratch Blog Page
Instagram: @Minnesotafromscratch Twitter: @StephLovestoCan

Mountain Rose Herbs: Mountainroseherbs.com
Excellent supplier of organic herbs in bulk.

ACKNOWLEDGMENTS

....

Thank you to the talented artist, Rhonda Asher, who drew the incredible colored-pencil section dividers throughout the book. They turned out even more beautiful and lifelike than I could have imagined. I'm honored you included your work in my book.

Thank you to Nicole Frail for believing in my book concept and making a dream come true. Thanks to both of my editors, Nicole Frail and Nicole Mele, for their support and guidance through this process.

Warmest thanks to all my family and friends who encouraged me to write this book, taste tested my experimental creations, and gave me feedback on my recipes. A special thanks to Grandma Elsie for sharing her mother's recipes with me, and to my friends Melanie and Joe Azen for going out of their way to offer so much help and support during the book-writing process.

Finally, thank you to my husband, Ben, and daughter, Sophia, who visited farmers' markets all around the state of Minnesota with me throughout 2016 and made countless store runs for this-or-that as I made magic in the kitchen. I appreciate your help through this process—and your help in the kitchen, too. You two mean the world to me; I'm so grateful for you both.

METRIC AND IMPERIAL CONVERSIONS
(These conversions are rounded for convenience)

Ingredient	Cups/Tablespoons/Teaspoons	Ounces	Grams/Milliliters
Butter	1 cup = 16 tablespoons = 2 sticks	8 ounces	230 grams
Cheese, shredded	1 cup	4 ounces	110 grams
Cream cheese	1 tablespoon	0.5 ounce	14.5 grams
Cornstarch	1 tablespoon	0.3 ounce	8 grams
Flour, all-purpose	1 cup/1 tablespoon	4.5 ounces/0.3 ounce	125 grams/8 grams
Flour, whole wheat	1 cup	4 ounces	120 grams
Fruit, dried	1 cup	4 ounces	120 grams
Fruits or veggies, chopped	1 cup	5 to 7 ounces	145 to 200 grams
Fruits or veggies, puréed	1 cup	8.5 ounces	245 grams
Honey, maple syrup, or corn syrup	1 tablespoon	.75 ounce	20 grams
Liquids: cream, milk, water, or juice	1 cup	8 fluid ounces	240 milliliters
Oats	1 cup	5.5 ounces	150 grams
Salt	1 teaspoon	0.2 ounce	6 grams
Spices: cinnamon, cloves, ginger, or nutmeg (ground)	1 teaspoon	0.2 ounce	5 milliliters
Sugar, brown, firmly packed	1 cup	7 ounces	200 grams
Sugar, white	1 cup/1 tablespoon	7 ounces/0.5 ounce	200 grams/12.5 grams
Vanilla extract	1 teaspoon	0.2 ounce	4 grams

Fahrenheit	Celsius	Gas Mark
225°	110°	$1/4$
250°	120°	$1/2$
275°	140°	1
300°	150°	2
325°	160°	3
350°	180°	4
375°	190°	5
400°	200°	6
425°	220°	7
450°	230°	8

INDEX

....